In memory of Dr Peter Brandon (1927–2011)
author of *The South Downs*

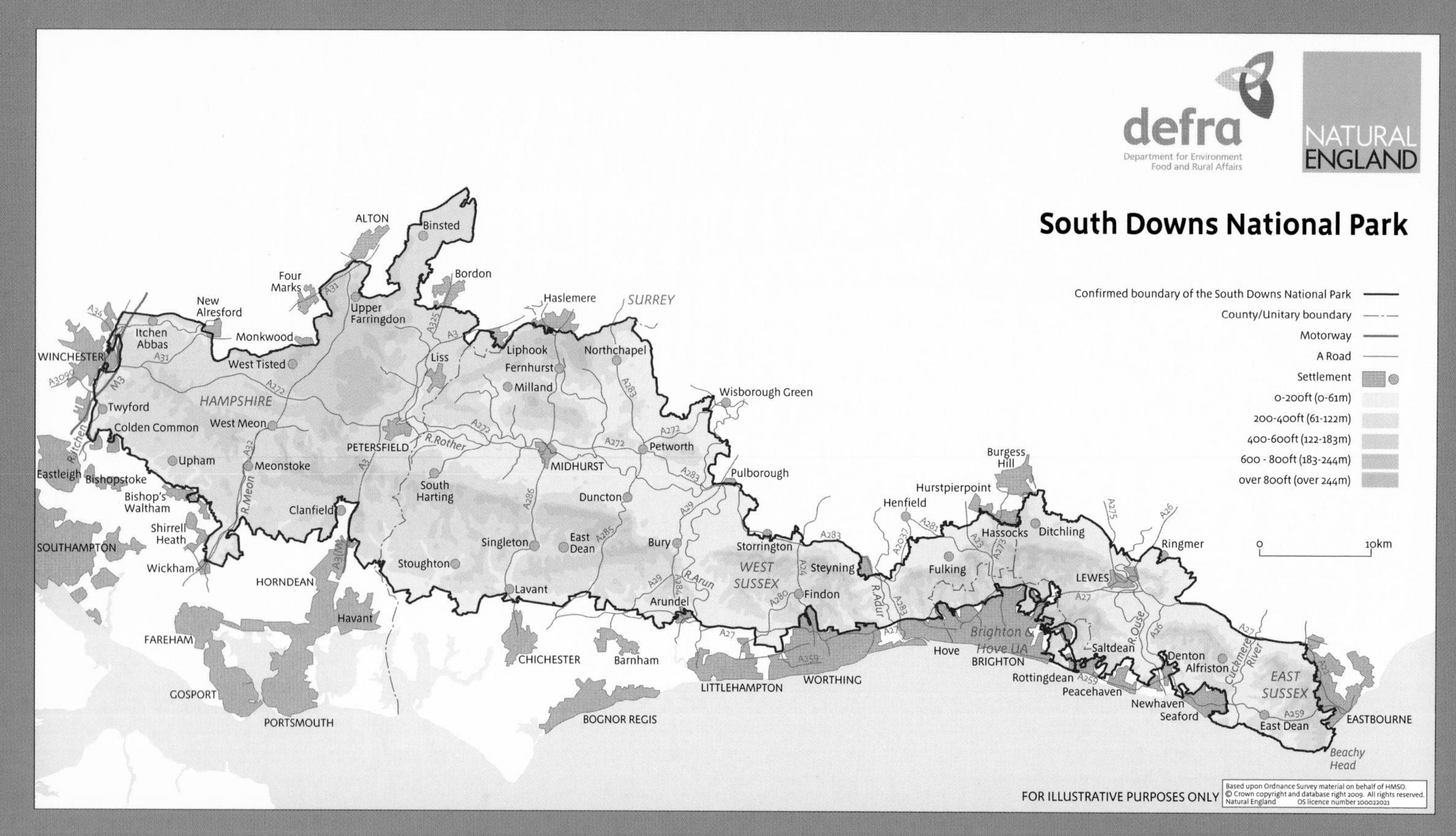

Map of the South Downs National Park showing the Park boundary, modern towns, major rivers and main roads. (Reproduced by courtesy of Natural England.)

The Archaeology of the South Downs National Park

An Introduction

by John Manley

ISBN 978-0-904973-22-8

Published by The Sussex Archaeological Society, Lewes

Typesetting by Dora A. Kemp, MPhil

Printed in Great Britain by Short Run Press, Exeter

Contents

Acknowledgements

This work is based on the efforts of generations of historians and archaeologists who have studied the past of the area now designated as the South Downs National Park, not least the endeavours of the person to whom I have dedicated this book. Their enquiries have made these pages possible. I would also like to thank the main sponsors of this book – the South Downs National Park Authority, a private benefactor, Jo Windsor, and the CEO of the Sussex Archaeological Society – they have all helped make the book a practical possibility. In particular I am in the debt of several people who commented on an earlier draft of the text: Professors Peter Drewett, Brian Short and Robin Milner-Gulland (University of Sussex), Dr Mark Gardiner (Queen's University, Belfast), David Hopkins (Hampshire County Archaeologist), David McOmish (English Heritage), David Allen (Hampshire Museum Service), James Kenny (Chichester District Archaeologist) and Casper Johnson and Greg Shuter (East Sussex County Council Archaeologists). Their collective critique filled in the many holes in my understanding and steadied my grammar. The illustrations come from a variety of sources, but I single out Russell Oliver and Simon Goodman especially for their emotive images. I would also like to thank particularly an old friend – Leslie Weller – for first introducing me to the great north scarp of the chalk downs on a clear and sunny summer's evening. My greatest gratitude I reserve for my partner, Lesley. Not only has she had to endure me typing at home for lengthy periods, but also the countless interrupted downland perambulations, when every little grass-covered hummock or building provoked enquiry, or worse, a digital photograph (or several). Sheltering with her on the Downs, in a thicket of gorse or hawthorn, watching the cloak of an unexpected shower drawing slowly across the Weald, brought welcome respite.

Brief explanatory note on chronology and dates

Please note that dates in this work are expressed with reference to the Common Era, either Before Common Era (BCE) or Common Era (CE). Thus 1805 CE corresponds to AD 1805 and 700 BCE corresponds to 700 BC. A small *c.* in front of a date stands for *circa*, meaning approximately.

Expressions such as 16th century or 18th century usually refer to the Common Era, unless otherwise indicated. So 16th century refers to the years 1501–1600 CE, and 18th century equates with the years 1701–1800 CE, and so on. In the 20th century the dates for World War I are 1914–1918, and for World War II they are 1939–1945.

Conventional archaeological and historic period labels are used sparingly in the text. For the sake of clarification the principal ones, relevant to the South Downs National Park, are provided here.

Period	**Approximate date range**
Palaeolithic (Old Stone Age)	450,000 BCE to 9000 BCE
Mesolithic (Middle Stone Age)	9000 BCE to 4000 BCE
Neolithic (New Stone Age)	4000 BCE to 2500 BCE
Bronze Age	2500 BCE to 700 BCE
Iron Age	700 BCE to 43 CE
Roman	43 CE to 410 CE
Saxon	410 CE to 1066 CE
Medieval	1066 CE to 1500 CE
Early Modern	1500 CE to 1750 CE
Modern	1750 CE onwards

The Archaeology of the South Downs National Park

On top of the world

For those of you who have already visited the undulating hills of the South Downs, you will know, whatever your mood, that it is hard not to feel exhilarated by the experience of standing on the edge of its precipitous north scarp, gazing out over the gently ribbed expanse of the wooded Weald. The naturalist William Henry Hudson wrote 'during the whole fifty-three mile length from Beachy Head to Harting the ground never rises above a height of 850 feet, but we feel on top of the world'. And it's true – we do (1). With shape-shifting fluffy clouds drifting across a blue sky, and the sun resting between your shoulders, you can really feel 'on top of the world'. But give yourself an additional treat. Walk along a little, and turn through 180 degrees. Just occasionally, across the stretches of downland to the south, you glimpse along a dry valley and a flat flash of blue appears on the horizon – the sun winks back at you from the English Channel (2). People have lived and visited the Downs for thousands of years. Did they have similar feelings when admiring these views, or not? Did they think the Downs were 'special'? There are some clues, and they lie in the traces they left behind. I want to help you discover them.

People have lived, hunted, farmed, worshipped, gathered together and buried their dead in the area now designated the South Downs National Park for over 8000 years. They continue to do so. Long before that time, human activity in the Park was intermittent, largely dependent on whether the cold episodes of the last Ice Age permitted occupation at all. The earliest human activity was discovered at Boxgrove, just on the southern boundary of the Park, north-east of Chichester. There, beautifully fashioned flint tools and animal bones indicate the presence of several families of hunters in the very remote past – it's difficult to imagine, but they were there around 400,000 years ago. Much more recently, by some 8000 years ago, the climate had warmed up considerably, and bands of people who lived by hunting, gathering and fishing came to the Downs and stayed. Human beings have been there ever since.

But before I introduce these people, it's important we get one thing straight. Despite its name – the South Downs National Park – the Park is not simply the chalk Downs, although these rounded hills, running in a continuous line from east to west, do constitute a sort of geological vertebrae. At the much larger western end, the Park extends considerably to the north to include the valley of the Rother with its lowland heaths, and then beyond to the sandstones and greensands that are much more dominant than in the east, and give rise to a distinctive feel for the landscape and vegetation. With hill-slopes supporting oak, hazel, ash and elm these sandstone ridges are famous for their 'hangers' – dense cloaks of tree-cover that cling tenaciously to their sides (3). And indeed, the highest point in the South Downs National Park is not on the

1. *(left)* It takes your breath away – standing on the north scarp of the Downs, looking out over the Weald. An old chalk quarry lies at bottom left, but your sight-line is inevitably drawn northward between the villages of Keymer (to the left) and Ditchling – and onto the ridge of the High Weald.

2. The folds of the Downs lie together in alternating ridges, creating patterns of sunlight and shadows. And just occasionally you get sight of the sea and the glinting white chalk cliffs that form the dramatic south-eastern boundary of the South Downs National Park.

3. The Hampshire 'Hangers' at Selborne – mature woodlands that cover the flanks of both chalk and greensand hillsides – a very different landscape to the downland grasslands to the south and east.

Downs, but at Blackdown (280 metres), south of Haslemere, where the sandstone supports dense stands of pine and a cover of heather.

The different groups of people in the area now designated the Park, over this very long period of time, have both exploited its natural resources and often left behind a legacy of their presence. They have quarried the chalk and mined the flint, hunted its animals, fished its bisecting rivers and collected its wild plants, berries, nuts and fungi. They have coppiced its woods, ploughed its fields and lined dew-ponds with clay to catch its rainfall. They used some of the resources – earth, timber, chalk, greensand, sandstone and flint – to build structures and craft objects to make their lives more comfortable and more meaningful. At various times they constructed houses to live in, of all shapes and sizes, from round to rectangular, from simple to grand. They sank fish-traps, pioneered trackways and roads, and constructed earthen banks around deer-parks; laid out ditches and hedges to surround fields, put up sheep-pens, built mills to catch downland winds to turn grain into flour (4), and brick-built mansions to supply water (5). In times of crisis great complexes of ditches and banks could be erected, or towering stone citadels to dominate and repel, and more recently brick and concrete installations to guard and defend threats from the air and sea.

4. The stilled sails of Jill (of the Jack and Jill windmills), south of Clayton, as dusk falls. The mills could be turned to face the wind,

5. Twyford Waterworks, a pumping station dating from the start of the 20th century, is situated at the western end of the Park, and comprises a unique collection of buildings and machinery. Chalk was quarried on site, burnt in lime kilns, and the resultant quicklime used to soften the raw well-water.

6. The Chattri (meaning 'umbrella'), above Brighton, is a strikingly singular monument. Inspired by the flamboyant Indian architecture of Brighton Pavilion, it marks the cremation pyre of Hindu and Sikh soldiers who gave their lives for Britain in the First World War.

But then, as now, life was not just about practicalities of existence. People built special places where they could meet in larger gatherings than usual, swapping stories, continuing old rivalries or finding partners. Places where they could joke, feast, gamble, compete, and generally enjoy themselves. To appease, enlist the support of, or worship ancestral figures or singular deities people resorted to a variety of activities which have left their mark, especially on the Downs. They gathered together to sacrifice objects, and bury them in the ground; they erected temples to all manner of gods; closer to our era they fashioned great places of communal worship – churches, chapels, monasteries and priories. And some people today venerate a chalk figure at Wilmington. Lastly, the Park area has been the final resting place for many. The thousands of prehistoric round earthen mounds or 'barrows' that must have once formed necklace-like lines along the imposing north scarp of the Downs, attest to places of mourning and memory, as do the tombstones of lower-lying medieval churchyards. Today the tradition continues – the Chattri Monument (6) north of Brighton commemorates the cremations of Sikh and Hindu soldiers who fought for the British. Clayton Wood, south of Hassocks provides a green alternative to traditional cemeteries, offering services for scattering of ashes and eco-friendly burials within sight of Jack and Jill windmills.

Very few regions on earth have all the resources that human beings, with their capacity for invention and imagination, require. Rich in chalk, flint and woodland, and with some well-drained, fertile soils – the Park region has few clay sources to exploit, relatively little workable stone for

7. The three grass-covered mounds on the skyline probably mark cremation burials dating to around 2000 BCE. The bank of the much later hillfort (left side of the main image) encloses a much larger area (see inset image), including the barrows. The hillfort builders left the mounds intact – perhaps out of a knowing respect for, or fear of, the dead.

building and no metal sources. Some of these things, therefore, had to be brought from both near and far: for building – greensand (predominantly at the western end of the Park), or quality limestone from Caen in Normandy. Clay for ceramics and bricks came from places such as Burgess Hill, just to the north of the Park, while iron-rich deposits were plentiful in the Weald. Museums, in and around the Park, are full of things that gave comfort and ultimately meaning to lives in the past – flint tools, ceramic cooking pots, bronze spearheads, iron fire backs, wooden furniture, all manner of textiles and clothing, tokens, jewellery and even golden rings declaring everlasting love. But not everything has found its way into museums. Even today, walking on broken downland ground, you may be lucky enough to spot a 4000-year-old flint scraper, that was once used to prepare an animal hide for a garment, its serrated edge still sharp, still serviceable.

The South Downs National Park therefore contains a long legacy of earthworks, buildings and objects left by previous generations. And each successive generation was faced by the challenge of what to do with the things it had inherited. Sometimes they simply neglected them, re-used them or deliberately destroyed them, but often they were more circumspect. For instance, the people who dug the great ditch around Old Winchester Hill (7) in the Iron Age drove their perimeter ditch through much earlier Bronze Age barrows. Almost certainly they knew these mounds were burial places of people long ago, and probably for that reason, inside their hillfort, they left intact another three very prominent barrows – it was a question of respect and veneration; perhaps compensation even for the dead they had disturbed. In like manner occasional finds of prehistoric objects by occupants of the region during the Roman period were treated with curiosity and kept for reverential reasons, or just simply as good-luck charms. The re-use of Roman bricks in Saxon churches suggests a more prosaic connection. And spare a thought, as your train speeds up out of Lewes station, Brighton bound, for the founders of Lewes Priory, William de Warenne and his wife Gundrada (see image 66). Their bodies were disturbed during the building of the line in 1845 and their remains laid to rest

8. A couple look southwards across the Chichester coastal plain and out to sea, from the southern side of The Trundle – a site that is both a Neolithic causewayed camp and a much later Iron Age hillfort. Some of its encircling earthworks may have once been more chalk than grass, and hence much whiter.

9. The Trundle showing the slight curving inner bank that marks the ditch of the causewayed camp.

(again) in the nearby church of St John the Baptist, in Southover.

In this short introduction to the archaeology of the South Downs National Park I want to pick out, highly selectively, some of the special places and sites left behind by past communities who have lived, hunted, farmed, worked or simply occasionally visited the region. I cannot produce here a comprehensive guide to all, or indeed even most, of the archaeological sites in the Park – a very large book would be required to do that. It will also become obvious to you that my 'archaeology' encompasses not only material remains from the remote past but also from the quite recent. To emphasise this theme I want to stress that there are some threads (as well as some ruptures) linking those families six thousand years ago who may have gathered at Whitehawk, above Brighton or The Trundle (8, 9), near Chichester – and ourselves. I will point out easily accessible monuments which you can visit, and tell you about some sites where traces of the past are hidden or have disappeared, and where your imagination will have to do the work. When you do so you can reflect on how the experience of being in the Park (admittedly an artificial construct that has little historical validity) once shaped past lives and now shapes yours (10). To that end, rather than set out the content of this book in chronological or geographical sections, I have opted to let each brief chapter tell the story of some enduring activities that transcend generational fault lines. To narrate a more meaningful and complete narrative of the past I occasionally wander outside the Park boundaries. But first I begin with stories from the earth itself.

10. The steep north scarp of the Downs west of Devil's Dyke. The earthwork centre-left is supposedly a Norman fortification – a motte and bailey known as Edburton Castle. In fact the castle-builders may well have used some earlier prehistoric barrows to give them a head start in construction. Further along the scarp lie Truleigh Hill (by the masts), Steyning (in the dip) and in the distance Chanctonbury Ring.

From the earth

Much of the rock beneath the resiliently springy turf of the South Downs consists of bands of white or greyish chalk, and nodules or horizontal slabs of black or grey flint. The chalk (which is a very pure form of limestone, up to 95% calcium carbonate) was deposited in extraordinarily different conditions from those we live in today. A warm, shallow tropical sea covered most of north-west Europe, between 70 and 100 million years ago. Chalk was formed by billions of slowly-sinking microscopic plankton, whose minute skeletons gradually amassed on the sea floor; the tiny white bones gave the rock its distinctive colour (11). However, the tectonic plates of Africa and Europe were inching closer together. Their eventual collision pushed up the Himalayas, the Alps and raised a chalk dome covering what we now call south-east England. Subsequent erosion weathered away the soft top of the dome, leaving the North and South Downs facing each other across the older clays of the Weald. The South Downs were gradually sculpted into discrete chalk blocks as river valleys were carved out by the Cuckmere, Ouse, Adur and Arun. In Hampshire, too, higher areas of chalk were isolated by the rivers Meon and Itchen. The combination of freeze-thaw-erosion cycles during the relatively recent Ice Ages weathered out some of the Downs' characteristic dry valleys, such as the celebrated Devil's Dyke north of Brighton.

11. From the air, the strikingly white scar of a modern chalk quarry punctures the springy turf cover on the west side of Wolstonbury Hill. Clever landscaping helps to hide the quarry from most perspectives on the ground.

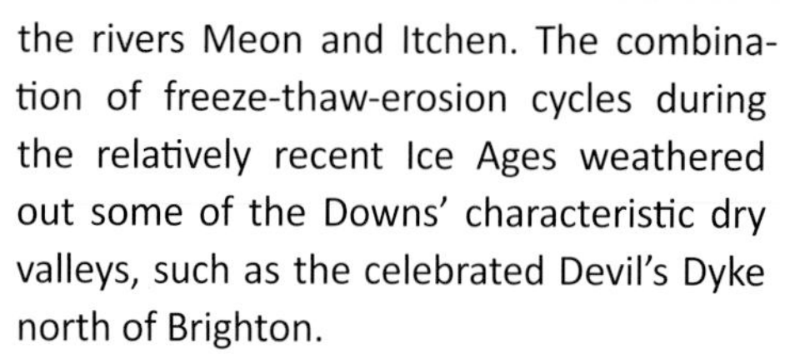

So much for the geological history. The real importance of the chalk Downs to early generations lay in its more obviously apparent features. The oldest chalk lies under the higher elevations of the north scarp, and from there it is possible to see across the Weald of south-east England, to the greensand hills of Surrey and the chalk of the North Downs. The lower rises and falls of the sands and clays of the Weald thus seem framed and encircled by a greensand and downland ring. It can be no coincidence that many of the major prehistoric monuments in the South Downs National Park were sited to make use of such sweeping views, and for the same reason the South Downs Way tracks the north scarp for much of its length. Underfoot, when wet, chalk paths turn to a cloying greyish mulch, but in the droughts of summer the chalk crumbles, so that driven cattle can kick up clouds of white dust behind them. It was this whiteness of the chalk that was also attractive to builders of earthworks. Those earthen banks around the many Iron Age hillforts, or the countless prehistoric burial mounds, now so deceptively grass-covered, blending into green backdrops all too easily, were once gleaming and white, beacons of light that shone out and defiantly marked their presence.

For much of the prehistoric period the black gold of the Downs lay in the tabular seams of flint layered within the chalk (12). Before the advent of metals, flint could be worked into all manner of tools for cutting, scraping, chopping, piercing and killing that were essential for everyday existence. The beauty of flint lay in its newly mined properties. Fresh from the chalk it has the consistency of hard toffee, broken and flaked with practised ease, using soft antler hammers. The presence of valuable flint must have been obvious to early communities. Any pit dug into the chalk was likely to produce the odd nodule, while observations of the chalk faces of the seaward cliffs of the Downs would have revealed thick seams of flint. Prehistoric people, of course, were not geologists or natural scientists. They were, however, deeply conscious of their dependence on the living plants and animals around them, and no doubt believed in forces beyond themselves, such as ancestors or spirits, who controlled all the materials they relied upon for life. The quality of the tabular flint, at such a depth into the chalk, would have seemed like the casual gift of a capricious spirit. To retrieve the prize would require dangerously deep digging, tunnelling and mining, while hoping that the ancestors and spirits of the underworld provided protection.

12. Near Newhaven, this chalk exposure has weathered to a creamy buff colour, but it still shows the horizontal bands of tabular flint. Once a shaft had reached a good layer of flint, radiating galleries could be excavated to follow the level seam.

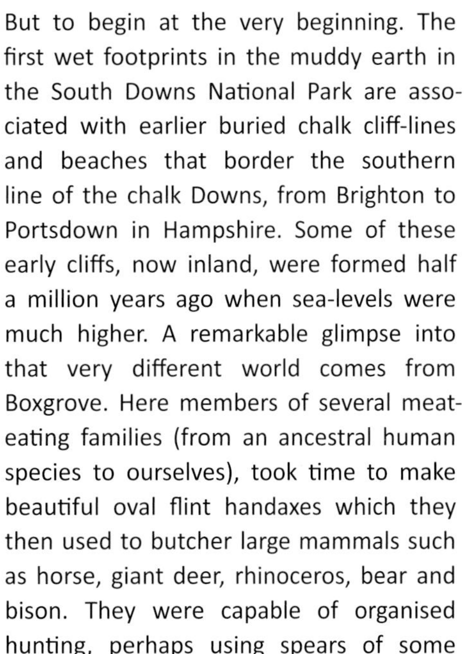
But to begin at the very beginning. The first wet footprints in the muddy earth in the South Downs National Park are associated with earlier buried chalk cliff-lines and beaches that border the southern line of the chalk Downs, from Brighton to Portsdown in Hampshire. Some of these early cliffs, now inland, were formed half a million years ago when sea-levels were much higher. A remarkable glimpse into that very different world comes from Boxgrove. Here members of several meat-eating families (from an ancestral human species to ourselves), took time to make beautiful oval flint handaxes which they then used to butcher large mammals such as horse, giant deer, rhinoceros, bear and bison. They were capable of organised hunting, perhaps using spears of some sort, and, in the absence of fire, may have eaten the meat raw. A fragment of human leg bone found at the site shows that these individuals must have been strong-limbed. They were living at the far extremity of human occupation at the time and intermittently retreated southwards when the climate cooled.

Flint was extremely important to the first hunters and gatherers who began to venture up onto the Downs from around 6000 BCE onwards, with the general warming of the climate following the end of the last Ice Age. These people (the same species as ourselves), probably comprised small bands of several families. They hunted deer, wild cattle and pig, and trapped birds and rodents. They caught fish, collected shell-

13. The flint head of a 'tranchet' axe from Pyecombe, north of Brighton. Perhaps used by early hunters and gatherers to clear woodland, it would have originally been hafted in a wooden handle. The word 'tranchet' comes from the French verb *trancher*, to cut, and refers to the oblique flake removed to form the cutting edge (right side of image).

14. A microlith means a small stone and you can see in this image just how minute a prehistoric microlith was. If you handle one you will see that these tiny triangular flint objects often have even tinier chips flaked off the edges, giving them a serrated feel. Inserted together in a line in a wooden handle they proved ideal tools to cut through light vegetation.

fish, dug up roots and tubers, and gathered nuts and berries. They fashioned garments from skins, baskets from plant fibres and erected shelters from branches and saplings. They probably moved around from seasonal camp to camp. And fundamental to all these activities was a complex toolkit made of axes (13) and differently shaped small pieces of flint, with keenly serrated edges – archaeologists call these microliths. Their campsites have been found the length and breadth of the South Downs National Park – from Bullock Down (behind Beachy Head) in the east, to West Heath (between Petersfield and Midhurst) and Selborne (in the north of the Park). Combinations of microliths may have been glued with birch resin (a black tarry substance obtained from burning birch bark) into wooden handles, making the first composite tools (14).

From around 4000 BCE farming lifestyles, based on the cultivation of cereals and the raising of cattle and sheep, gradually replaced and marginalised hunting and gathering. Flint was important to the first farmers of what is now the South Downs National Park but some of it was extracted in a wholly different way. Unlike their hunter predecessors, who had obtained flint from small pits, surface scatters, beach cobbles or river gravels, the first farmers mined the deeply layered flint, leaving a series of remarkable mine shafts, underground galleries, spoil dumps and working areas at several sites in West Sussex, such as Harrow Hill, Church Hill, Long Down and Cissbury (15). The mines seem to have been excavated using picks fashioned from deer antlers and shovels made from their shoulder blades, and the flint from them was largely used for the manufacture of axes, perhaps for the purpose of clearing trees for fields, or for exchange with neighbouring communities. Despite the better quality of mined flint, there is plenty of circumstantial evidence to suggest that the dangerous deep mining of flint may have had a social and ritual significance, as well as a functional motivation. Enigmatic chalk objects and incised lines on the walls of some galleries, plus occasional human burials and individual human bones, coupled with the fact that surface flint was readily available, argue that there was something in the very prestige of this difficult task that encouraged people to excavate. The scale of mining was small, and episodic; perhaps only one or two shafts were open at any time. However, the occurrence of paired shafts raises the possibility that occasional flint mining was a ritualized and competi-

15. The western end of the later prehistoric hillfort at Cissbury is pocked by a series of moon-like craters which mark an extensive series of filled-in prehistoric flint mine-shafts. These depressions mark the first 'industrial landscape' within the South Downs National Park.

16. This curious piece of sculpted and incised chalk was found in The Trundle causewayed camp. Its original shape is unknown, but it is assumed that it once formed a complete circle with a large, central perforation. In its current, fragmentary state it looks uncannily figurative, as if depicting a garment or cloak, draped around the shoulders of some prominent individual.

tive practice. In addition, there may have been something prized in the very colour of mined flint. The quest between competing kin groups may have been more important than the buried quarry.

The materials of chalk and flint are very different. You can saw, cleave and sometimes carve chalk into manageable blocks (16), but the stone itself is soft, porous and weathers easily. Some of the harder chalks, occasionally referred to as clunch, can be used for internal walls not exposed to weathering (17). An important characteristic of chalk, thanks to all those billions of dead plankton, is that it is alkaline, making it an ideal material to reduce the acidity of some soils, breaking up heavy clay soils and allowing manure to penetrate more effectively – thus making them more fertile. Flint, on the other hand, can be flaked into flat or sharp shapes, although it can snap and break; otherwise it is water-resistant and durable – well suited for use in external walls and foundations. Most or all of these qualities were probably known to people throughout prehistory. And it is not surprising therefore, that those master-builders the Romans, who constructed most of the earliest stone buildings, or at least stone foundations, in southern Britain realized the different building materials on offer in the South Downs National Park. At Fishbourne Roman Palace, constructed in the late 1st century CE, the foundations comprised layered and mortared courses of roughly squared flint, with facing stones from the local greensand, quarried from north of the South Downs, where it occurred in a line from Bignor through Petersfield. Chalk was conspicuous by its absence.

17. These walls are all that remain of the 13th-century Dominican Priory at Arundel. The chalk facing on the internal wall can be clearly seen, as can the flint on the external walls, and the use of greensand around the window.

18. Flint and greensand are used to chequer-board effect on the facade of Marlipins, a 12th-century building in Shoreham-by-Sea, just outside the South Downs National Park. The building houses an important collection documenting the maritime history of the area.

19. Flint and greensand are often used to complementary effect in standing buildings. On the corner of the Norman gateway at Lewes Castle, greensand quoins provide the neat right angles for walls primarily composed of angular flints.

Throughout the South Downs National Park many important medieval and later buildings were constructed from combinations of local building stone: flint, greensand, chalk and occasionally other varieties of sandstone. Randomly shaped 'boulder' flints can simply be laid in irregular patterns to make field boundary walls, while rounded cobble flints can be mortared in neat horizontal rows. Knapped and squared flint can be used for facing stones, sometimes forming startling patterns like the chequerboard facade of the medieval building of Marlipins, Shoreham (18), or deployed to stylish effect as in the 18th-century two-storey stables at Goodwood House. Flint was not good for making corners, and these were often managed through the use of squared greensand, or building stone from the Isle of Wight or imported from Caen in Normandy (19). Chalk was much more frequently used as the internal rubble make-up of walls or for their inside facing. In the north of the Park, around Selborne, a belt of greensand, known locally as malmstone, is accessible and can be seen in the facades of many buildings, formed by regular or irregular courses of this creamy-coloured stone. Brick and tile, dug, moulded and baked from the clays of the Weald, gradually complemented stone-work from the 16th century onwards. Only a minority of buildings were made of stone, of course. Humbler buildings utilised clays for cob and daub walls, timber for roof purlins and furniture, and dried grasses for roofing thatch.

The earth thus provided tools for our earliest ancestors and, more recently, stones and organic materials for buildings, roofs, furniture, utensils, containers, gates and fences. But wandering through the South Downs National Park you will stumble on tell-tale signs of how the earth has provided the ingredients that helped other vitally important processes. The white gash of an old chalk quarry, particularly along the north scarp of the Downs, is testimony to the extraction of chalk not only for building but also for quantities of lime for use in construction, especially from the 18th century onwards (20). Chalk can also be burnt in kilns to produce lime to assist agricultural fertility. Farms often had their own kiln in the corner of a field built for that purpose. The north scarp of the Downs is occasionally scarred diagonally by deep cuts that run down its flank, providing the trackways or 'bostals' for the movement of chalk, lime and animals.

20. These lime kilns were erected at Amberley Chalk Pits in about 1905. Railway platforms on each side of the block of kilns allowed the transfer of lime (used for mortar and agricultural use) directly from the kilns to railway wagons.

21. The Beeding Cement Works near Shoreham which closed in 1991. The chalk quarry actually dates back to 1851 and cement was manufactured on the site from at least 1898. A tunnel under the road separates the distribution plant and administrative blocks (west) and the industrial site and chalk quarry (east). Chalk from the local quarry was an essential material for the production of cement.

The remains of the recent past can be just as moving as those from earlier times. The abandoned Beeding Cement Works (21), once a major employer making cement from the local chalk, now lies eerily quiet, its austere facades pierced by rows of broken windows. Finally, across the South Downs National Park extensive coppiced woodlands provided vital fuel for the production of charcoal, used in the Wealden iron industries in the 16th to 18th centuries, by itinerant charcoal-burners. Making charcoal in makeshift kilns was a slow and unpredictable process, sometimes lasting up to five days, and occasionally leading to rapid deforestation when no replacement plantings were made. But for the charcoal burner, in his hut, the long nights tending the fire resulted in a commodity that others would pay for.

The earth of the South Downs National Park therefore provided some of the raw materials with which generations of communities could provide homes and furniture, tools and fuel. But the mainstay of existence, food, drink and clothing, conjured up from the natural resources of the area, remained a constant preoccupation – from those first families at Boxgrove to the 21st century. Let's look for some tell-tale signs people have left behind in their constant quest to stay fed, watered and warm.

Hunting, fishing, farming ... and conservation

The archaeological evidence for diet is slight and often uncertain, and we need to use our imaginations to put flesh on the bone, quite literally. As the climate warmed some 8000 years ago, a patchy woodland of oak, hazel, lime, ash and elm spread throughout the area now designated as the South Downs National Park and it was into this kind of environment that the first bands of hunters and gatherers, groups of several families, set up seasonal camps. They may have used flint axes and fires to open up and enlarge natural clearances in the scrub and woodland, thereby attracting grazing animals such as deer, perhaps fed with ivy by the hunters, wild boar and wild cattle. At Iping Common in West Sussex, on the greensand, pollen evidence recovered from an excavation suggests deliberate opening up of a hazel woodland to establish clearings of heather-covered heathland. Hunted animals provided not only protein but also bones for tools, skins for clothing and containers, and sinews for cordage. Their only truly domesticated animals were dogs, no doubt employed to help with hunting and fetching quarry. Other foods came in the form of nuts, berries, wild grasses and fungi; hazelnuts were particularly favoured. Fishing and shellfish complemented the diet.

Studies of surviving hunters and gatherers in other parts of the world have provided some useful stimuli for our imaginations, although we must be wary of over-generalization. What they do show is that hunters and gatherers in our area may have been self-sufficient with only a few hours of 'work' per day; that they may have been quite egalitarian, with no fixed leaders and few material goods, with women undertaking most of the gathering and men doing the hunting. They also point to small groups of people who had an intensively knowledgeable appreciation of all the living things in their environment, who knew both how to 'manage' them, and most importantly, to 'sustain' resources for the future. Their relationship with the landscape, and with the things that grew and lived there, was probably overridingly mystical, as is suggested by the ceremonial deer-masks found at a broadly contemporary site of Star Carr in North Yorkshire. They were part of nature, not above it. However, we must be wary of portraying our early ancestors as happy bands of wandering and well-fed environmentalists. There were, no doubt, plenty of quarrels and disputes, occasional inter-band aggression, seasonal food shortages and a life expectancy much shorter than our own.

The fundamentals of diet gradually changed around 6000 years ago, beginning with the arrival of some groups of people, and some new-fangled ideas, from the near Continent. They bought with them the resources for rudimentary farming – domesticated animals such as cattle, sheep, goat and pig, and cereals; and the first cooking vessels (22). Larger clearances were made on the Downs by the newcomers, but for a long time, perhaps more than 2000 years, the land-

22. This round-bottomed pot was found at the causewayed camp of Whitehawk, above Brighton. The first farmers, arriving from the near Continent, brought the first domesticated farm animals, such as cattle and sheep. They also brought knowledge of potting, and made vessels used for cooking, as well as eating and drinking.

scape of the Downs would have been a mosaic of woodland and seasonally-cleared grasslands for pasture and planting (23). At Bishopstone, at the eastern extremity of the South Downs National Park, evidence has been found for prehistoric ancestors of modern cereals, such as emmer wheat and six-row barley, as well as possible food plants like fat hen, burdock and chickweed. Shellfish collecting continued – with mussels, oyster, cockle and limpets in abundance.

Again, it's time to use our imagination. How did these newcomers relate to the indigenous hunters and gatherers? Studies elsewhere suggest that, although these lifestyles are very different, hunters and farmers can exist in proximity and usefully exchange products and services that each group is more skilled at acquiring. They can also intermarry – leading to socially intertwined relationships as well as 'economic' ones. Without taking the analogy too far, you might imagine that the patchwork of woodlands for hunting and gathering, and farmed, seasonal clearances might symbolize the social arrangements of communities of hunters and farmers living in close proximity. That closeness, however, may have brought its own problems of misunderstandings, petty thefts, trespass, animal rustling or worse.

23. The first farmers needed to clear trees to make way for fields and pasture. This is a pre-form (or 'rough-out') for a flint axe from Cissbury. This one was probably discarded because of some defect. Finished examples would be polished and hafted in wooden handles.

Over the long term, there is something inherently unstable in the relationship between ways of life dependent on hunting and those reliant on farming, although farmers often still engaged in hunting, especially in times of food shortages. Recent colonial history demonstrates the rapid marginalization of those American Indians or Australian Aborigines who relied exclusively on hunting, gathering and fishing. While the transition in our region was nothing like as rapid, eventually the gradual restrictions placed on hunting and gathering by the growing numbers of farmers, improving agricultural technology, and the larger size of their herds and clearings would have led inexorably to an accelerating reduction in the 'wild' landscapes left for hunting and gathering. The archaeological evidence is both clear and dramatic – the first permanent rectangular fields, surrounded by hedges and banks, appear on the Downs some 3500 years ago. Two enclosures at New Barn Down, on the block of downland between the Arun and the Adur, are linked to a system of rectangular fields and trackways. An animal or storage structure and a quern stone remind us of the farming necessity of storing harvested produce to feed both animals and humans over the winter. Another example of the permanence of farming settlements and their fields is the complex at Plumpton Plain, where field-systems stretch south-east from the main centre of habitation. It is a wonderful place to visit – with views south-east towards the sea, and the north escarpment and Wealden views a short walk away (see image 35). And finally, the southern flanks of Butser Hill, just south of

24. If you were a farmer you needed to keep grain dry over the winter for future consumption, or as seed corn for the following year. This is a reconstruction of a 'four-poster' from Butser. Many people think these were used as family granaries.

25. These hanging chalk loom-weights keep woollen threads tight on this reconstructed upright loom from Butser. The production of woven and dyed garments must have been an activity common to many settlements.

Petersfield in Hampshire, are covered with an impressive network of prehistoric rectangular fields, seen clearly from the air as a lattice of boundary earthworks, or lynchets.

Climate change, so threatening for the contemporary world, has occurred before. The onset of the Iron Age, about 700 BCE, coincided with a much damper environment, further intensifying the environmental pressures on farming communities. Such were the consequences that population numbers may have shrunk for a few generations as increased rainfall, soil erosion and flooding rivers made some land unusable. The surviving downland communities who emerged from this disaster invested in protection, not only for themselves but for their herds and agricultural surpluses. A four-post timber structure (24) at Park Brow, just north of Cissbury Ring, set amongst fields, may have been a small granary. Surrounded by a protected landscape of palisades, fields and trackways, finds of spindle whorls, loom weights and a weaving comb, although known in previous centuries, attest the need to keep warm and dry (25). A settlement further west above Chichester at Lavant, guarded by the nearby hillfort of The Trundle, contained round buildings, an iron sickle (26) and a series of four-post granaries for storage.

An agricultural revolution occurred when the area now occupied by the South Downs National Park was incorporated into the Roman Empire. New foods arrived with

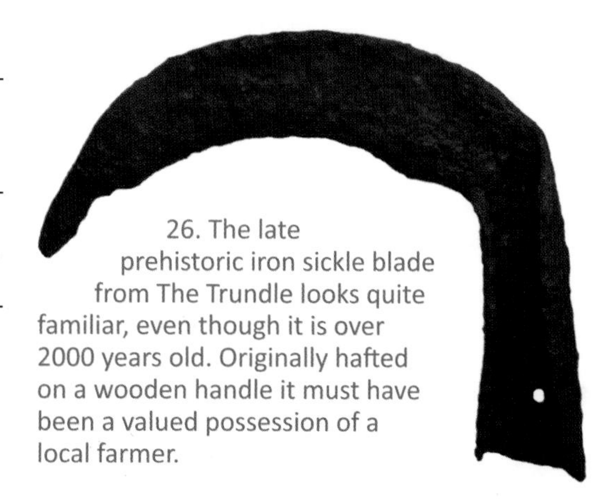

26. The late prehistoric iron sickle blade from The Trundle looks quite familiar, even though it is over 2000 years old. Originally hafted on a wooden handle it must have been a valued possession of a local farmer.

Roman administration, and new tableware with which to serve them (27). There were classic Mediterranean imports such as figs, olives and grapes. Additionally novel fruits and vegetables were introduced and became integrated into the local agricultural system, such as domestic apples, pears, plums, cherries, walnuts, lettuce and leeks. It was not all good news for the conquered. The Romans introduced taxation on a widespread scale – both in agricultural kind and in cash. As a result new field-systems proliferated (e.g. at Thundersbarrow above Shoreham, and at Jevington in the east of the Park), and greater yields were demanded from older prehistoric fields. A corn-drying oven at Bullock Down, near Eastbourne, two corn-drying kilns at Thundersbarrow and no less than eleven such kilns attached to an aisled barn at West Blatchington in Hove indicate the pressure on farmers to increase outputs.

The collapse of the Roman Empire meant that market-orientated agricultural practices disappeared. Population declined and subsequently Saxon newcomers settled amongst the surviving locals in the South Downs, sometimes living in one place for a few generations then relocating (as at Chalton in Hampshire). They mostly practised subsistence farming geared towards feeding local kin rather than producing a surplus for exchange. At Bishopstone, near Newhaven in East Sussex, cereals were grown on fields attached to the settlement, while animals included sheep, cattle, pig, horse, red and roe deer, geese and fowl. Bones from conger eel and whiting show that resources from the sea were also not ignored. These settler societies had simple, subsistence concerns as the few finds of whetstones, spindle whorls and pottery from a typical rectangular sunken-hut at North Marden (north of Chichester) indicate. However, towards the end of the Saxon period, the impact of Christianity, and the growth of aristocratic estates, both secular and religious, led to the rise of high-status settlements founded in new locations. Again at Bishopstone, but this time founded close to the extant Saxon church, a cemetery, then a privileged settlement developed (see image 42). The inhabitants fed on pig and marine fish, as well as red deer, roe deer, hare and badger. Land organisation and agricultural tributes from those who worked the land were designed to support conspicuous consumption and 'hospitality feasting' by those at the summit of local social hierarchies.

27. *(inset)* This Roman bowl recovered from the sea off Beachy Head reminds us that the Romans not only introduced new foods but also new objects to serve them on, and eat them with. It is also underlines the importance of trade by sea.

28. One of the largest aisled barns in Sussex at Alciston, east of Lewes. Built on medieval foundations it was originally constructed for the Benedictine monks of Battle Abbey on their estate at Alciston, and was used to house wool, hay and corn.

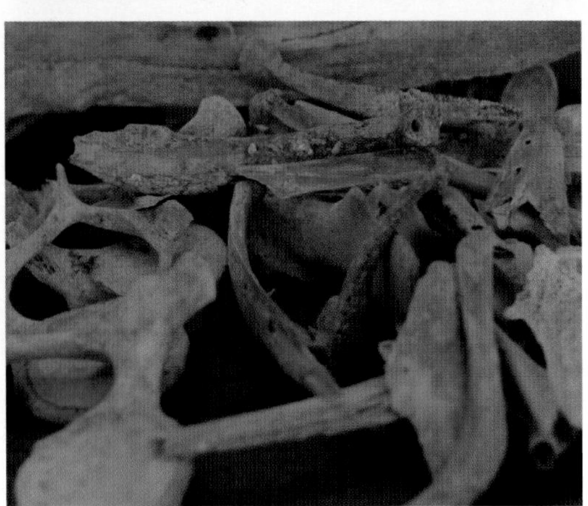

29. The slight remains of a medieval deer-park pale, consisting of bank (foreground) and ditch (grass in the background) at Marwell in the south-western end of the South Downs National Park. Deer hunting provided exclusive and elite sport for both men and women, while peasant poachers were ever-present.

30. Porpoise bones from Lewes Priory, on display at Barbican House Museum, Lewes. These bones reflect the high-status diets of leading medieval clerics. Porpoise apparently could also be dried and still retain its taste.

By the Norman Conquest of 1066 the Sussex half of the South Downs National Park was divided into administrative areas known as 'rapes'. There were six in all, each controlled by a castle, such as Arundel, Bramber and Lewes. They formed the foundations of a feudal system of lay and ecclesiastical estates (28) for exploiting the labour and produce of peasant farmers. The downland landscape was home to a mosaic of economic practices, from extensive sheep pastures (more common in the east), some open fields, aristocratic forests, deer parks (29) for hunting (more common in the west, where plentiful trees facilitated both the observation of deer and concealment of the stalker), rabbit warrens (bred for their fur and meat) and the consumption of high-status foods from the sea (30) or closer-to-home fishponds (31). The ubiquity of sheep farming on the Downs in the medieval period was closely linked to the cultivation of fields. A three-course rotation was often employed of autumn wheat, spring barley and fallow. Sheep, kept largely for their wool, were looked after by solitary downland shepherds during the summer and used as moveable manure heaps to fertilize the crop-yielding soils at night. Hazel stands, coppiced on a seven-year cycle, supplied the portable hurdles for managing large flocks (32).

31. These fishponds provided fish for the extensive household at Bishop's Waltham Palace. Excavated in the first instance to breed fresh water fish such as bream and pike, carp became increasingly more popular after their introduction in the late 14th century.

32. A hazel coppice in Sussex. Hazel is inseparable from history. Its multitude of uses included thatching, firewood, hurdles and furniture, as well as nuts for food. In the past hazel was also credited with magical powers – a hazel rod protected against evil spirits while a nut could be worn as a charm to ward off rheumatism.

Throughout the last 1000 years the Park landscape was shaped by social and political changes taking place on the national and international stages. The slow erosion of the manorial system of farming, with peasants tied to the land of their Lords, the emergence of parishes, the break-up of large ecclesiastical estates following the English Reformation of the 16th century, and the success of the iron-making revolution in the nearby Weald radically changed ways-of-life. The onset of more 'rational' ways to farm, inspired by the Enlightenment of the 18th century and the emergence of large, industrialised cities also opened up new opportunities. Wealthy aristocrats constructed 'great houses' complemented by large estates (especially in the western section of the Park). Inspired by the age of 'scientific' discoveries they brought fresh ideas to downland farming. Innovative fodder crops for sheep, such as swedes and turnips, imported initially from the Continent, were planted. A famous improved brand of sheep was bred on the Downs, the Southdown. Celebrated for its quality of wool, it was claimed that live wool on the back of a sheep in the morning could be tailored into a gentleman's coat by the evening (33). The growing industries elsewhere in the country, and the masses of workers required by them, eventually led to a greater demand for meat from sheep.

33. These sheep were grazing at Milland, within the Park on the Sussex/Hampshire border. Centuries of breeding have now resulted in hundreds of different breeds. These are typical Southdown sheep, producing high-quality wool for garments. They are also used in cross-breeding to produce fast-growing meat lambs and to clean up any arable prior to sowing.

34. Tourism, outdoor pursuits and casual visits provide the incentives for many visitors to the South Downs National Park. In some areas, where access is confined, as here south of Clayton, it can get quite busy!

The 20th century also brought significant changes to downland life. Political ideologies and two world wars impoverished most of the great country houses, leading to the breaking up of many remaining estates, and the ploughing of more extensive areas of downland to feed a post-1945 population living off rations. Mechanisation in farming led to rural depopulation and the post-war creation of large downland fenced fields, covered in cereals, presented the casual visitor with a more restricted landscape, and undermined earlier attempts to create a National Park. However, the emergence of middle-class tourism brought new visitors to admire the sweeping downland scenery, and the momentum for recognition of the special qualities of this landscape gathered renewed pace (34).

But it is time to retrace our steps. Having looked at how people obtained food, drink and clothing from the territory of the Park we now want to see what kinds of buildings they constructed to shelter themselves from the elements, and, importantly, how they sometimes used them to show off their status to the neighbours.

Living buildings

The archaeology of buildings doesn't have a great deal to tell us for the earliest part of human occupation in the South Downs National Park. The last hunters and gatherers, who camped on the Downs between 8000 and 6000 years ago, discarded flint tools but left no traces of their dwellings (or at least none that have been discovered yet). From evidence elsewhere the circular or oval structures would have been made of wood and covered with organic material such as skins. Part of the reason for their non-discovery is that they would have been relatively flimsy since they were designed to be not only lived in, but carried, too, from seasonal camp to camp. Nor do we have much better luck when we look for the houses of the first farmers on the Downs, who grazed their cattle and planted crops from 4000 BCE onwards. Again, by analogy elsewhere archaeologists should have found at least one or two rectangular timber buildings, their wooden posts rotting and leaving post-holes in the ground. There should be long-houses, for extended families, and perhaps byres for animals or storage, especially as the South Downs National Park is one of the richest areas for other types of monument constructed by the early agriculturalists. These buildings lie hidden somewhere, but where? Some people argue that they lie concealed at the bottom of valley sides, underneath metres of agriculturally-disturbed soil washed down through the ages.

The earliest domestic structures that lie within the South Downs National Park appear associated with the first signs of intensification of farming, represented by the small, rectangular fields, dating to around 3500 years ago. Small, round, timber buildings, with wattle and daub walls and thatch roofs cluster together in downland farmsteads, often surrounded by palisades or embankments. Let's look at two excavated examples, Black Patch and Itford Hill, to the east of Lewes. At Black Patch a number of circular huts were discovered associated with an extensive system of fields. The huts were constructed on terraces levelled into the sloping hillside. Five huts were excavated, along with nearby fence-lines and ponds. Artefacts within the huts suggest that some were used for sleeping in, others for flint knapping, lambing or storage. The social structure of the occupants is notoriously difficult to reconstruct from archaeological remains but it is possible that polygamy was practised and some of the huts were for ancillary wives. Alternatively they could have been for siblings or grandparents. Itford Hill is similar to Black Patch, sited on a southward facing downland slope, with fields to the south. The latest interpretation of the site suggests that the settlement started with two houses, which expanded to five, then shrank to three and finally two. It is very tempting to think that these fluctuations mirror the number of family residents, swelling as children are young, shrinking as they grow to adults, find partners and leave, perhaps to found their own settlement. Similar farmsteads have been excavated at Plumpton

35. Slight grass-covered banks and ditches comprise the remains of a Bronze Age farming settlement above Plumpton, on the Downs. Surveys have demonstrated that a system of fields and trackways existed to the south-east of the site.

Plain (35) and further west at New Barn Down, above Worthing. In Hampshire an extensive area of unenclosed occupation was revealed at Easton Lane, near Winchester. Here, ten circular post-built structures were found, along with numerous other buildings, pits, ditches and burials. Other potentially contemporary sites are suggested for Chalton and West Meon.

During the much wetter Iron Age, from 700 BCE, circular timber houses, perhaps slightly larger, were the main house type. The best example from Sussex is near Lavant, at a site called Chalkpit Lane. An unenclosed southward-facing settlement of up to thirteen round-houses, complete with four-, six- and eight-post granaries was excavated. There were some rudimentary indications of planning at Chalkpit Lane, with the houses seemingly distributed either side of a communal open space, facing each other. The other interesting thing about this site is that the settlement boundary was not located and it is conceivable that there is an extensive complex of round-houses, perhaps thirty or more, at this location, just south of The Trundle hillfort. At Winnall Down, near Winchester, eight circular structures and other features were surrounded by a bank and ditch.

36. A collection of replica Iron Age round-houses nestles below a chalk ridge near Chalton in Hampshire. Experiments conducted at the site, especially in terms of the construction and use of round-houses, have provided significant insights into prehistoric life.

What was it like to live in a round-house? Luckily you can visit the Butser Ancient Farm, just south of Petersfield, and look around one of these houses yourself (36). For the modern visitor there are often two concerns, the lack of 'privacy' and the 'smoke gets in your eyes' problem. In a large round-house, with effectively only one large round room, (although screens could be put up to at least provide visual privacy), how could you do anything 'in private'? The key to answering this issue lies in realizing that our concept of 'privacy' is a very modern one. In the ancient world, for instance, domestic slaves often slept in the same bedroom as their masters and mistresses. Visitors always ask about cooking over hearths in the centre of round-houses, and the fact that no round-house has a chimney. In practice the smoke from a central fire curls gently upwards to the conical roof, and slowly escapes through the thatch, killing lots of little bugs as it does, and thereby prolonging the life-span of the house (37). Many of these late prehistoric round-houses faced south-east, towards the rising sun, probably both for religious and functional reasons. Imagine the light streaming in through the door in the early morning, lighting up the southern sides of the house and moving around the walls towards the north in the early afternoon. The daily journey of reflected sunlight on the internal wall of the round-house mirrored the travel of

37. This is pretty much the view you would get if you fell asleep around the central hearth in an Iron Age round-house. Note the absence of a vent to let out the smoke. In practice the smoke just dissipates through the thatch, driving out small pests and keeping the roof as dry as possible.

38. The reconstructed Roman villa at Butser. By contrast with the adjacent cosy round-houses, the villa feels rather cold and impersonal. But the villa did have windows and a corridor running its entire length, which allowed the creation of several separate rooms.

the sun across the sky, emphasising the cyclical aspects of rural lives.

Fundamental changes in living buildings occurred when the Park region and southern Britain were incorporated within the Roman Empire. While most people continued to live in round-houses, a few adopted new ways of living in rectangular buildings, some of which, in the countryside, are described by archaeologists, rather grandly, as 'villas'. You can visit an excellent reconstruction of part of a villa (one that was excavated at Sparsholt, near Winchester) at Butser (38). The differences between this structure and the round-houses are obvious. The tiled roof, lime-washed walls and windows are all things that don't feature in circular houses. But the really big differences lie within. There are several separate rectangular rooms of varying sizes (allowing status differences to emerge between the inhabitants), a flanking corridor and a hypocaust (under-floor heating system); many villas also had communal baths. You don't have to be an archaeologist to imagine the different attitudes of the people who lived in villas. They were interested in making a statement about their status, enjoyed some degree of privacy and had novel attitudes about decorated floors and the use of hot water for bathing, as evidenced from surviving villas at Fishbourne (39) and Bignor (40). They also may have owned slaves, who, in some cases, slept in traditional round-houses, no doubt located discreetly to the rear of the main building.

By the end of the Roman period, while Roman towns, such as Chichester and Winchester were in decline, some villas in the countryside witnessed their greatest period of prosperity. You can see for yourself just how grand some villas had become by visiting Bignor Roman Villa, south of Petworth on the fertile greensand ridge in the shadow of the north scarp. In its final form, the villa consisted of some sixty-five rooms surrounding a courtyard, with a number of outlying farm buildings. The latest phase of building involved additions to the north wing, and it is here that most of the fine mosaics are located. The reconstruction of

39. A guided tour taking place at the remains of Fishbourne Roman Palace, near Chichester. In the background is a mosaic with its central round panel featuring the famous cupid-on-a-dolphin scene. Depictions of dolphins appear frequently on Roman mosaics.

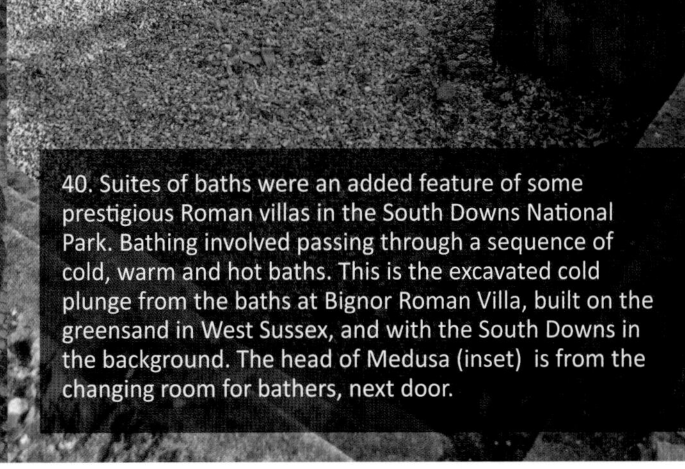

40. Suites of baths were an added feature of some prestigious Roman villas in the South Downs National Park. Bathing involved passing through a sequence of cold, warm and hot baths. This is the excavated cold plunge from the baths at Bignor Roman Villa, built on the greensand in West Sussex, and with the South Downs in the background. The head of Medusa (inset) is from the changing room for bathers, next door.

the facade of an aisled barn at Meonstoke shows just how sophisticated some agricultural buildings had also become (41). The collapse of the western Roman Empire brought those lifestyles to an end. The economic infrastructure that supported monetary exchange for building products and craft workers who designed and laid elaborate mosaics slowly disintegrated. Security in the countryside disappeared and Saxon newcomers took full advantage. The next living buildings to appear in the South Downs National Park went back to basics.

Saxons migrating to Sussex from northern Europe brought with them the tradition of thatched timber building. Two types of structure predominate in these early villages, rectangular buildings used for occupation and small sunken-floored huts that were probably used for a variety of craft activities, including weaving. These type of settlements have been found along the length of the South Downs National Park, from Bishopstone in the east, to Botolphs by the river Adur, West Marden north of Chichester, Chalton on the Hampshire Downs and Shavards Farm, Meonstoke. There is a concentration of early Saxon finds between the rivers Ouse and Cuckmere, and it is possible that the late Romano-British people granted lands here to the Saxons in return for tribute or services of some kind. However, equally early Saxon graves have been found at Eastbourne. Some of the Saxons were not averse to living in the decaying ruins of Roman villas, like Beddingham, near Lewes. Other families must have been quite fearful as they wandered past crumbling Roman buildings, noting the tumbled stone walls, gaping roofs, spaces now colonised by animals, birds, and no doubt at night, ghosts.

41. This reconstruction, based on archaeological evidence, of an aisled barn at Meonstoke in Hampshire demonstrates the sophistication of some ordinary buildings during the Roman period.

By the later Saxon period population growth and an increasing diversity of economic practices, including exchange and trade with the near Continent, led to the emergence of different settlement types. At Botolphs, in the Adur valley, rectangular timber buildings, on east–west and north–south alignments, were built over the early Saxon settlement. At Bishopstone, the late Saxon settlement buildings, this time on a different site to their early Saxon predecessor, but with the same orientations as Botolphs, were laid out to the north of a Christian shrine and early church. They included a remarkable cellared structure that probably supported a tower, suggesting a distinctly high-status site in the countryside (42). During this period, in the 10th and 11th centuries, the Park's first towns (since the Romans left that is!) were being founded. Steyning, near the Adur north of the Downs, and Winchester in the west are two of the foremost examples (both just outside the Park's boundaries), along with the *burh* underneath modern Lewes established in the time of King Alfred. Rows of rectangular buildings, and newly-laid streets, along with evidence of metalworking and the minting of coins, reveal embryonic urban elements in a still dominantly rural landscape.

The new Norman overlords were intent on maximising the tax returns from the countryside, either in kind or coin, as that nation-wide tax assessment document, Domesday Book, indicates. Both the settlements in the countryside which formed villages, and nascent urban sites around new Norman castles, continued to grow in numbers. Indeed the 13th century saw a period of expansion when marginal land within the South Downs National Park was taken over for farming and the establishment of small villages. However, a combination of several factors, including the emparkment of land for hunting by the rich landowners, and the Black Death of the mid-14th century, led to the desertion of hundreds of these outlying villages, forming the phenomenon that archaeologists call Deserted Medieval Villages. Often these comprised no more than a single street, with timbered and thatched buildings either side, a small church and perhaps a Manor House and a mill. You can still walk along the deserted and grassed streets, and over the small rectangular house plots, of some of these pioneering agriculturalists. Abandoned villages were once populated at Perching, above Southwick, at Monkton, north of Chichester, Abbotstone near New Alresford, Beddingham near Lewes, and further examples existed at Colemore and Priors Dean in East Hampshire. In some cases it is tempting to conjure up an idyll of rural life, but in reality, under the watchful eyes

42. An impression of the late Saxon settlement at Bishopstone, near Newhaven. Note the enigmatic tower-like structure and the early church (top right).

43. The regimented facade of Uppark House, built in 1690 and rescued after a disastrous fire in 1989. This is a classic 'upstairs/ downstairs' house and the Victorian servants' quarters are complete with tunnels in the basement of the house.

44. Petworth House is probably the stand-out stately home in the South Downs National Park. Built in the late 17th century it sits in a deer park landscaped by England's greatest gardener – Capability Brown. The house is open to the public and contains the National Trust's finest collection of paintings.

of the Lord of the Manor's bailiff, the daily grind must have been long and hard.

At the other end of the social scale, the break-up of large ecclesiastical estates such as those of Lewes Priory and the Bishop of Winchester – the latter one of the wealthiest in England – during the Reformation, and their sale by the Crown into private hands provided opportunities for the elite to build grand country houses, often surrounded by hunting parks and landscaped gardens. The larger aristocratic houses are concentrated in the middle section of the South Downs National Park and include such properties as Uppark, Stansted and Wiston (43). One of the grandest is Petworth House (44), rebuilt in 1688 by Charles Seymour, 6th Duke of Somerset, and altered in the 1870s by Anthony Salvin. The site was previously occupied by a fortified manor house founded by Henry de Percy, the 13th-century chapel and undercroft of which still survive. In the east lesser large houses, those of the well-off gentry, included Danny and Plumpton. The majority of these houses were of two or three storeys, often laid out in an 'E'- or 'H'-shaped plan. The Hampshire village of Chawton is famous for having both Chawton House, an Elizabethan manor house and home to Jane Austen's brother, Edward Knight, and a large 17th-century house where Jane Austen herself spent the last eight years of her life (45). Many of these grand homes survived into the 19th and early 20th centuries, from time to time hosting the highest echelons of society (Edward VII enjoyed West Dean enough to make several visits). These large estates were also home to hundreds of estate work-

45. The 17th-century brick house was the home of novelist Jane Austen for the last eight years of her life. She died in 1817. In this solid-looking village house she wrote the novels *Mansfield Park*, *Emma*, and *Persuasion*.

46. These are workers' cottages in the parish of Beddingham, east of Lewes. The cottages in the photographs were built in 1867/68 for the labourers in the local chalk pit. They were built by the Weller family of builders, brick and flint layers and dew-pond constructors, who were based in Pear Tree Cottage, next to Glynde shop.

ers and their families, who sometimes lived in purpose-built accommodation on-site and spent their entire lives as part of the estate community. Relations, and occasional tensions, between the estate aristocracy and its workers are now, of course, the stuff of televised English costume dramas.

The living buildings of the modern period comprise a mix of old and new. In the towns within the South Downs National Park older timber-framed medieval houses were provided with a Georgian make-over, with its emphasis on a frontage pierced by evenly spaced windows, providing an overall geometric effect. The rising numbers of the middle class constructed fine Victorian and Edwardian houses lining suburban streets. The new wealth of industrial entrepreneurs spawned enterprises in the countryside that needed numbers of workers to turn a profit. The more enlightened, perhaps more canny, operators built rows of workers' cottages close by, ensuring that if workers were late, they could be found easily. An example of such housing was built at Tidemills, east of Newhaven, and on the Glynde estate, near Lewes (46). In Hampshire in the late 19th century the gin merchant William Nicholson built a lot of properties in and around Privett for his workers at the Basing Park Estate. The consistent architectural form and style of Nicholson's buildings is what gives Privett its individual character, which included gables, flint with brick dressings and decorative stones such as Nicholson's own crest and initials.

Rising population numbers in the 20th century meant that the need for new, lower-cost, housing was paramount, much as it still is today. The settlement of Peacehaven, on the

47. The Yeoman's House, situated near Bignor in West Sussex, dates from *c.*1420 and is a fine example of a medieval hall-house. A composite facade made from flint, brick, leaded-lights and lime-washed panelling is held together by a sturdy timber framework, and capped by an impressive thatched roof.

chalk downs some six miles east of Brighton, was a novel, and controversial, planned town in the 1920s. A grid of roads (running east–west) and avenues (north–south) created plots for some relatively poor housing, occasionally fashioned from ex-army huts or old railway carriages. Notwithstanding its controversial beginning Peacehaven has contributed in its own way to the history of the area, if only by serving as a warning about the dangers of poorly designed buildings. Hence its location just outside the Park. It now supports a flourishing local history society, and has notably featured in recent literature and drama, including *Brighton Rock*, *Mr Bean* and *Eastenders*.

Living buildings provide shelter and warmth and their diverse characters, materials and history provide an obvious reminder of past livelihoods within the South Downs National Park (47). However, people are instinctively social, and there is little doubt that they were equally so in remote prehistory, quite likely even more so. And much of social and communal life takes place 'outdoors'. The first great gathering places were marked out on the Downs nearly 6000 years ago. It's time to travel back and find out what they were talking about.

Meeting places, meeting people

Ever since the first people arrived in our area they met other people from time to time, and gathered together in larger groups. It is easy to think that these occasional gatherings were prompted by the need to co-operate in some functional activity. For instance, some 8000 years ago hunters and gatherers may have banded together to clear patches of woodland, or organise themselves so that they could more easily stalk a herd of deer and perhaps drive one into an ambush where it could be killed. The resulting amount of meat, far too large for a small family to consume, could be shared out amongst the wider group. But there were other, more sociable, reasons why people concentrated occasionally in one place. They could exchange information, seek out partners, conduct a variety of rituals relating to life-cycle events, such as births, coming-of-age ceremonies, marriages, or deaths, give and receive gifts, share out food, feast and party, decide on questions of right and wrong, compete for status and group approval, gamble and drink, or just discuss the weather. In many ways these are some of the things that we still do today when we go to meeting places.

The places where hunters and gatherers congregated to tell stories around camp fires have not survived for us to see today. Archaeological finds, however, demonstrate that plenty of them would have sat around cooking hearths on the greensand ridge, to the north of the chalk scarp, or the heathlands of the Rother valley. A combination of light woodland, hazel trees and especially nuts, and well-drained sandy soils made them ideal locations for seasonal or permanent camps. But you can visit some of the meeting places of the very first farmers within the South Downs National Park, who began to manage the landscape for cattle and sheep, and for crops. These were the direct but distant ancestors of downland farmers today. These meeting places are described by archaeologists as 'causewayed camps' and most date to around 6000 years ago. They are found on the Sussex Downs (as well as elsewhere in England), but with no known example (yet) in the Hampshire section of the South Downs National Park, including the greensand areas. These places must have been built by the first farmers who came from the near Continent, bringing livestock and cereals with them. They

48. Curious sheep are now the most frequent visitors to the causewayed camp at Barkhale, West Sussex. The nearest sheep stand on the slight earthwork bank that once circled the site, while the thistles in the foreground grow over its accompanying ditch. From the air (inset) – the layout of the site is clearer – two round barrows were built close to the camp at a much later date.

49. Four concentric rings of chalk bank and ditch once encircled the causewayed camp at Whitehawk, above Brighton. This reconstruction drawing shows people coming to the site from various directions, accessing the site by its many entrances or 'causeways'.

50. The causewayed camp at the end of the world, that's what being on Combe Hill feels like. Situated at the eastern end of the chalk ridge it enjoys panoramic views across Pevensey levels and the low Weald. Snow lies in the ditch with part of the curving bank inside it. On the horizon is the slight rise of a later round burial mound, or barrow. And another barrow (inset) lies immediately to the west.

are circular monuments, defining spaces some 200 metres or more in diameter. Their boundaries, often concentric, are formed by banks and ditches through which there are many 'causeways', hence the name. They were often built in places where there had been no previous human activity, suggesting these were 'neutral' or special places, distant from where people ordinarily lived. Examples in Sussex include The Trundle (above Chichester), Barkhale (48) on the north scarp near Bignor Hill, Whitehawk (49) (above Brighton) and Combe Hill (50) (above Eastbourne). In Hampshire a small circle of pits was discovered and excavated at Winnall Down (just east of Winchester). The pits contained four red deer antlers, some pieces of pottery and flint flakes. This site could also have functioned as an early meeting place, but is quite dissimilar to the 'causewayed camps' further east.

51. Some of the best-preserved round barrows within the South Downs National Park are at Devil's Humps, Kingley Vale, near Chichester. These massive burial mounds have encircling ditches, and often depressions in the centre, caused by antiquarian excavators. Not to be confused with the equally impressive barrows at Devil's Jumps, near Treyford (Midhurst). Both groups should be visited!

What took place at these meeting places? The broken pieces of pottery and artefacts, and fragments of animal and human bones found in some of the ditches of these 'camps' are capable of many different interpretations. Some people have suggested that each of the separate sections of ditches, divided by causeways, were in some way 'owned' by a particular family or kin-group. The activities that have been proposed for the meeting places range from feasting, to making and exchanging artefacts, from carrying out rituals to occasional human burials. Just as important, if not more so, were activities like those outlined at the start of this section, which have left behind no archaeological traces. These sites were special as *places* but they were also special at certain *times* of the agricultural year. It is quite probable that the leaders of communities only allowed these gatherings to take place at specified times, for instance, in late summer after any crops had been harvested, or before winter when surplus young cattle were sacrificed and consumed.

Meeting places changed location and form from century to century. The great number of burial monuments within the South Downs National Park – the earthen mounds called 'long barrows' and 'round barrows' (51) – provided particular places where people congregated, not only in the act of burial itself, but also subsequently, to commune with the dead and ask protection from the ancestors, as well as communicate with one another. There are also some hints that certain settlement locations could also function as meeting places. Just to the north of the 3000-year-old settlement of Itford Hill (near Lewes) was an isolated circular timber structure, quite possibly roofed, with an entrance to the south. Inside, under a pile of flint, lay the cremated remains of an old man, and outside were the cremated remains of at least eleven men, women and children. This looks like the grave of the man who founded the adjacent settlement, and the descendants of a number of such settlements could have met here to honour their founding father. Roughly contemporary with Itford is a very distinctive enclosure on Highdown Hill, near Worthing (52). It stands apart and seemingly in front of the main chalk ridge of the Downs, making it an obvious landmark for those further along the coast, or approaching from the sea. Bronze axes, chisels, knives and a gold ring found at Highdown show that one of the prominent activities at this meeting place was exchange.

This exchange was probably more akin to our own custom of giving presents on particular occasions, rather than acquiring new stuff through payment in kind. People at meeting places both gave and received things, sometimes even before they talked. In many cultures the act of exchange, between strangers who may not even share a language, is the first act of communication, of making a possible foe a probable friend. In the

52. Highdown Hill, near Worthing, although by no means the steepest or highest within the South Downs National Park, is one of the most prominent, certainly when viewed from the coastal plain or sea. On a clear day you can see eastwards to the chalk cliffs of the Seven Sisters. The image shows the earthwork bank on the south side, with a wide ditch beyond.

53. The hillfort at Hollingbury sits atop a small hill and now enjoys a view down to Brighton and the English Channel. Excavations in the 1930s showed that the earthen bank surrounding it was once vertically faced by timbers. Outside the fort the most prominent earthworks are those of the greens and bunkers belonging to the golf club.

prehistoric period it is quite likely that social ties between people of different communities were cemented through receiving objects from their neighbours. When they took gifts back to their homes, they took with them something of the giver, both materially and spiritually. The meeting places of the Iron Age in the South Downs National Park were undoubtedly the great hillforts dotted along the chalk ridge, from St Catherine's Hill east of Winchester to Hollingbury above Brighton (53). Within these encircling earthen banks, people congregated from time to time, giving agricultural tribute to their chiefs and spiritual leaders – the Druids – conducting rituals and sacrifices, giving and receiving gifts, adjudicating between rights and wrongs, bartering livestock and perhaps slaves. The vital social glue, however, that underpinned all these activities, and made people feel that they belonged to a community, was the sharing of the significant and the trivial: how to perform a proper sacrifice, or how to address a Chief; gathering together to witness significant performances, but also the indulging in gossip, shows of affection, spiteful rumours, competitive trials of strength and fortune-telling.

When southern Britain was incorporated within the Roman Empire the new administrators tried to encourage an urban way of living amongst some of the local population. Towns were founded at Winchester and Chichester (54), and smaller settlements such as Neatham, near Alton – all just outside the Park. The meeting places in these towns were known by the Latin word *forum* (pl. *fora*). At such places justice could be administered, disputes resolved, taxes collected, goods traded and bought, and both local and Roman gods honoured. But most of the population were not of continental origin and could trace their origin back to forebears in the Iron Age. It is not surprising, therefore, that a number of rural shrines were founded, such as at Lancing, and Bow Hill (above Chichester) where local gods could still receive sacrifices, and some of these were even sited within the ancient hillforts (e.g. Chanctonbury). A detached polygonal building close to Stroud Roman Villa at Petersfield may be an example from Hampshire.

Under the Saxons the area of the South Downs would have been divided into 'hundreds', which served as taxation and administrative units. The 'hundred' in theory was supposed to contain 100 'hides', a variable measure of taxable value linked to an area of land. The meeting place of the hundred court to administer justice and regulate local affairs was usually sited on a notable landmark, often a prehistoric monument such as a round barrow. One such example may be the Hundred Moot of Willingdon, on the Downs near Eastbourne. They could also be sited at the centre of an estate, or on neutral territory between estates. The frequency with which trade and exchange took place at such meeting places gradually increased their importance as markets. There were about 40 such hundreds in Hampshire, including those of East Meon, Selborne and Meonstoke within the South Downs National Park. Before the Norman Conquest of 1066 the increase in commercial activity, allied to maritime trade and the periodic need for defences, led to meeting places emerging in growing towns or *burhs*, many of them ports, where the minting of coinage had become established. Early towns included the ports of Lewes, Steyning and Arundel, as well as the administrative and ecclesiastical centres of Chichester and Winchester.

Buying and selling were closely controlled during the Middle Ages, and the Lord of the Manor had to obtain a grant to hold a market in his local town. Grants given were normally for a weekly market and perhaps a three-day annual fair. Trading came under

54. The town walls of Roman Chichester, complete with bastions added in the later Roman period. Connected by a network of roads, towns were places for people to congregate and trade. They were also places where the colonial authorities could administer justice, collect taxes and demonstrate how a Roman ought to live.

55. Commerce and prayer are surprisingly common bedfellows. On a rather gloomy Saturday morning in Petersfield colourful garments contrast with the stonework of St Peter's Church. A typical market square and a timeless scene.

56. This rather gaunt market cross identifies the market place in Alfriston in East Sussex. The only other indicator is the much wider road space at the centre of the village. Alfriston is an immensely attractive example of a downland settlement.

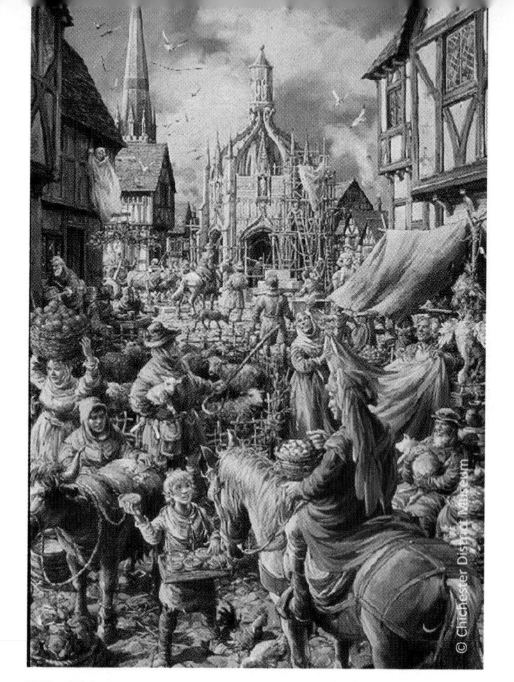

57. This is a reconstruction of the market cross in Chichester, right in the centre of the city. Erected probably during the time of Edward IV in the 15th century, it was constructed of Caen (Normandy) stone and apparently designed to provide a space where poor people could sell their wares.

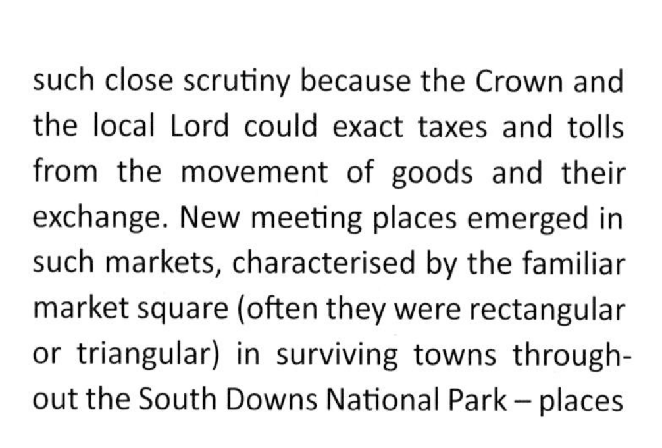

such close scrutiny because the Crown and the local Lord could exact taxes and tolls from the movement of goods and their exchange. New meeting places emerged in such markets, characterised by the familiar market square (often they were rectangular or triangular) in surviving towns throughout the South Downs National Park – places such as Alfriston (granted market rights 1406), Findon (1261), Harting (1271), Petersfield (1232 (55)), Meonstoke (1247) and Selborne (1270). The market at Bishop's Waltham, the site of a palace and town of the Bishop of Winchester, was in existence by 1273 and demonstrates that ecclesiastical as well as lay Lords could benefit from taxing trade. Markets often contained market crosses, such as those at Alfriston (56) and Chichester (57) and market halls, the former to mark the sites where trading could take place, the latter originally timber-framed buildings, raised on pillars. The open ground floor provided shelter for stall holders in foul weather, especially those selling perishables like butter, while the upper floors were used for administration. A fine example is that from Titchfield, near Fareham, now on display within the Park at the Weald and Downland Museum (see image 104). Annual fairs on the Downs were often agricultural in nature. Sheep were driven in large flocks to fairs, such as the one at Findon, where an annual three-day fair was in existence as long ago as 1261 and survives to the present.

Market trading was thirsty and tiring work, and every market square was soon surrounded by a number of alehouses and inns – the new meeting places, the 'pubs' which many of us are so fond of! Beer was one of the most common drinks, consumed by all social classes, and it also supplied much of the required daily calorific intake. The 'public houses' provided food, drink, beds and stables for horses. There are any number of examples scattered throughout the South Downs National Park such as The Bricklayers Arms (Midhurst), The White Hart (Lewes), The George (East Meon and also Alfriston (58)) – all bearing witness to the innate and enjoyable need for people to meet. During the Industrial Revolution of the 18th and 19th centuries, brewing was a very important industry, second only to cotton, and

58. The George Inn at Alfriston was first licensed in 1397, although the foundations of the building date back to about 1250. According to its publicity, there is a network of smugglers' tunnels leading from its cellars, and the South Downs Way passes its front door – which is, of course, quite convenient.

before the advent of widespread domestic lighting and reliable water supplies, most sociable activities, and even meetings concerning parish administration, took place in the 'pub'.

If pubs constitute the first stirrings of what has come to be known as the leisure industry then the discovery of the curative powers of sea-water provided the frenzy. The later 18th century saw the recognition of the supposed medicinal qualities of bathing in the sea, leading to the development of seaside resorts, such as Brighton, and encouraging great numbers of people from places such as London to cross the Downs by horse and carriage, and from the mid-19th century by train, to reap the benefits of the seaside. The first generations of visitors to the coastline of Hampshire and Sussex probably did not appreciate the quality of the downland landscape, but by the late 19th century, tastes had changed, and the quintessential qualities of the area, allied to growing interests in natural history and antiquities, led to the increasing popularity of the Downs. There was, however, a considerable discrepancy between the

59. You sense that the hillfort at Devil's Dyke on the north scarp of the South Downs has always been a popular spot. The earthen banks of the fort enclose a space that was more recently used as an early fun-fair, a military store, later for a pub, and most recently as the launching place for para-gliders. Dog-walkers, joggers and mountain bikers add to its colourful visitors. The inset image shows the Iron Age bank (left) juxtaposed with a 20th-century military store.

60. One of the latest meeting places just outside the Park, at Falmer, north of Brighton. Trackways and earthworks enclosing special spaces have now been replaced by the railway and the new Amex Community Stadium. We find some prehistoric practices baffling, but time-travellers from the past would struggle just as much understanding us – and the games we play.

poverty of some farming downland lives and the comparative wealth of those who could afford to escape the urban grime and enjoy the rural scenery. The historic legacy of this early tourism is still with us today. You can just about make out some of the remains of an early fun-fair on Devil's Dyke (59), as well as enjoy horse racing at Goodwood and Brighton, cricket at Petersfield (on a pitch surrounded by prehistoric burial mounds) and polo at Cowdray. More recent activities on the Downs include innumerable golf courses (e.g. West Meon) and para-gliding at Caburn (Lewes) and Old Winchester Hill (East Meon). The most recent manifestation of the need for humans to meet occasionally in larger groups must be the Amex Community Stadium (just outside the South Downs National Park) home to the Seagulls, Brighton and Hove Football Club (60).

The long and convoluted ancestry of meeting places, from causewayed camps of 6000 years ago to the Amex Stadium of 2012, is threaded together by the need for human beings to meet, gather, greet, and forge relationships in common undertakings. It has always been thus. Another shared and enduring characteristic is the need to believe in powers beyond the everyday. It is those forces that I now want to summon.

Beliefs, rituals and religions

Members of past communities in the South Downs National Park have always felt the need to believe in some external powers in addition to the forces under their immediate and obvious control. The hunter some 8000 years ago needed to be able to predict where herds of deer might shelter, or ensure that a carefully laid fish-trap was sufficiently enticing. Early pastoralists and farmers wanted newly-born calves to struggle to their feet quickly, or the sun to warm the soil, tempting forth green shoots from the seed. The first metallurgists shaping copper then bronze tools, and finally iron implements, sought guarantees that their smithing furnaces would be hot enough to make metal malleable but not brittle. So much in daily lives was unpredictable, so much outwith human control, that help was needed in the form of a body of beliefs and rituals that could tell the future and improve the chances of successful outcomes. Good and bad spirits could live anywhere, on the tops of the Downs, in clearings or in woodlands, in quiet dry valleys, in storm clouds and heat haze, in ponds, rivers and wells, and in pits underground. They could inhabit all manner of live things – from human witches to animals, fish, insects and flowers. They could lurk in useful objects – axes, arrowheads, quern stones, windows and doorways – as benevolent or malevolent forces or capriciously fluctuating between both. And they could be concealed in the unusual. Fossils such as sea-urchins are sometimes found on the Downs. Known as shepherds' purses, up to the 19th century they were thought to be good luck charms (61). But the burial of a woman on Whitehawk causewayed camp some 6000 years ago, complete with a pair of sea-urchins, tells us that such things were credited with special powers millennia ago. There were a lot of spirits and they were everywhere – during night and day, sleep and awake. You could converse with them or curse them, placate or annoy them, but in the long run you needed them on your side to survive.

61. Fossil echinoids, or sea-urchins, are found in the chalk. These examples can be seen in Horsham Museum. In recent times they used to be known as 'shepherds' purses' but the discovery of two sea-urchins in a grave at Whitehawk indicates that they also were valued some 6000 years ago.

Surmising from anthropological studies of surviving hunters, the first hunters who lived in the area of the Park no doubt undertook numerous rituals and made plentiful offerings to ensure a successful hunt. They apologised to the trees they felled with their flint axes in order to make woodland clearings. They murmured quiet spells when they laid clumps of ivy in the cleared spaces as fodder for deer. Crouching down in concealed hollows they called forth the spirits of the deer herd to offer to them one animal that could be sacrificed. When that animal was killed by multiple hunting arrows the hunters were both excited but also grateful for the gift received. Offerings of plants and berries were left behind by way of thanks. It was important that a relationship of goodwill was maintained between hunter and hunted, gatherer and gathered. Hunting wild boar, hooking fish, trapping birds and rodents, and returning to harvest protein and fat-rich hazelnuts were always activities where a little luck was needed.

From around 4000 BCE a different direction was given to subsistence activities, with more emphasis on pastoralism and agriculture, and a gradual need to identify more closely with certain fixed places in the landscape of the Downs. Some of these were the causewayed camps, noted above, and represented in Sussex by sites such as The Trundle and Barkhale in the west, and Offham and Combe Hill in the east. At some of these meeting places we can detect the traces left over from a number of rituals. First there is ample evidence for feasting, and feasting usually implies celebration and thanks – witness Thanksgiving Day in the United States and Canada, or its European equivalent, the Harvest Supper. There are also other indicators – a carved bone phallus from The Trundle might be interpreted as a fertility or good luck token, or something to ward off the evil eye. From the same site a carved chalk block (see image 16) with a spoke-like decorative pattern could be an attempt to depict the sun, or a feathered cape around the neck of a shaman or other ritual leader. At Offham, near Lewes, a pit contained the smashed fragments of a pottery bowl, a flint leaf-shaped arrowhead

62. This is a crouched burial of a young man, 20–25 years, found in the bottom of the causewayed ditch at Offham Hill, outside Lewes. People must have believed there was something special about this man, either in life or in death, since only a few individuals were ever buried in causewayed camps.

and bones from deer, cattle, pig and beaver. The deliberate and violent breaking of any made object is usually a sure sign of something abnormal. There are any number of possible reasons, but if this pottery bowl was used to contain ritual substances, it may have been deemed too dangerous for mortals to re-use, hence its deliberate concealment. A crouched human burial from Offham of a young man found in the ditch

63. Spearheads, a fragment of a gold torc or neckring, and this decorated armring were deliberately buried in the ground at West Ashling, north of Chichester, over 3000 years ago. They may have constituted an offering to a particular deity, perhaps requesting its intervention in daily life.

of the enclosure is suggestive of another common type of belief – that of the power of ancestors, or witches (62).

Copper and bronze weapons and tools appeared in the South Downs National Park in slowly increasing numbers from around 2000 BCE. Copper and bronze implements were prized items, manufactured away from settlements using esoteric and seemingly magical expertise, from materials initially won from the earth. Despite how odd it now appears to us, some of these desirable artefacts were surrendered back to the earth, buried in deposits that archaeologists call ‘hoards’ (63). Such a

64. The hill known as Mount Caburn is a distinctive landmark outside Lewes. Made into a hillfort in the late prehistoric period, the main activities or rites at the site at that time seem to have culminated in the deliberate burial of objects or part-objects in pits in the ground.

term implies safe-keeping and potential later retrieval, but the reality was that some of these hoards were given to be kept safely by the spirits of the underworld forever. Many such hoards were buried on dry ground but often close to rivers, pools and springs, arguing that some kind of water-deity might have been revered. Find-spots occur from Buriton and Langrish in the west to Firle and Iford in the east. There were a number of metalwork deposits close to the source of the Rother. At Buriton, a palstave (a type of bronze axe) was found on the edge of a steep-sided valley cut into the greensand, close to another spring. There is a cluster of three finds at Langrish, two of which are on sloping ground where water collects at the junction of the chalk and greensand. At Bramber, where the Adur cuts through the chalk, a Late Bronze Age hoard contained ninety-eight items (mostly spearheads), together with human and animal bones, burnt flints, pottery and possible crucible fragments. The deposit had been placed in marshy ground.

In the ensuing Iron Age, the centuries before the Roman Conquest, beliefs and rituals still seem to have involved the breaking, some of which was deliberate, and burial of objects in the ground. Within the hillfort of the Caburn, just east of Lewes, more than 140 pits contained a whole host of different objects, including weapons, iron knives, weaving combs, loom weights, broken quern stones and occasional human jaw bones (64). Since the Caburn does not seem to have been a permanently settled occupation site, the impression is that people were intermittently climbing up that steep hill, carrying broken or complete artefacts, to bury them at the climactic moment of specific rituals. What were these rituals for, and who were they aimed at? Conceivably there was a vast pantheon of underworld deities honoured through such practices, or perhaps the spirit lay within the artefact itself, the specific comb, knife or weapon. A specimen offered by way of ritual sacrifice may have increased the earthly power of the artefacts that remained. At The Trundle myriad small pieces of broken quern stones were found in pits, too small to be the result of accidental breakage. Do these suggest offerings to a fertility deity, deliberate sacrifices, or the intentional burial of a worn-out but respected object that had 'died'?

During the Roman period in the area now designated the South Downs National Park there was a concentration of rituals and religion in the first built structures that could be described as 'temples'. Examples occur at Lancing, Slonk Hill (Shoreham), Chanctonbury Ring (65) and Bow Hill (above Chichester) and at Hayling Island, to the south of the Park. However, these are not the classical multi-columned buildings found in the Mediterranean world, but small square, circular or polygonal buildings that owe much to local conceptions of construction methods and building forms. The gods worshipped in these places were probably a conflation of classical deities and Iron Age gods. Worship is probably the wrong term. The numbers of coins found at some of these sites demonstrates that there was something mercenary about human/divine relationships. You made offerings (i.e. paid) for the intervention of particular gods, and if they proved ineffective, you probably went to another temple. Some of the characteristics and practices at these temples – their siting within Iron Age hillforts, and the burial of ox and pig skulls – suggest some continuity of indigenous ritual practice. Rituals and religious beliefs are never uniform in any society – there are always variations of practice, and sometimes completely contrary notions of what constitutes proper forms of worship. Lastly, there is more than a hint that some of these 'temples' were the destinations

65. The hillfort of Chanctonbury on the north scarp of the Downs in West Sussex is one of the iconic landmarks for those walking the South Downs Way. In the Roman period it was a religious centre, as evidenced by the construction of two temples within the earthworks.

for pilgrimages. Their out-of-the-way but highly visible locations (Hayling Island, Bow Hill, Chanctonbury) strongly suggests that the effort people made in getting to them was part and parcel of their veneration.

The Anglo-Saxons introduced a variety of pagan practices to communities in the Park area, not least in terms of burial rites. Saxon religion drew on its Germanic homeland and Iron Age traditions. It was polytheistic in character, and also revered supernatural entities which inhabited the landscape, such as elves and dragons. Worship took place at regular festivals and involved the sacrifice of inanimate objects and animals. There are hints of such practices at the later Saxon settlement of Bishopstone (Newhaven). Although the elite at Bishopstone were nominally Christian, the remains of animals in pits appear to be from pagan rituals. Christianity eventually spread throughout the Park region, suppressing overt paganism, with the creation of Bishoprics at Winchester and Chichester and the establishment of Minster Churches, the predecessors of later parish churches. For example, Minster Churches existed at Winchester, Chichester, Singleton, Arundel, Steyning, Lewes and probably Bishopstone. New religious establishments after the

66. Normans ruled both by the power of the sword and by the power of prayer. This image depicts Lewes Priory, in origin a Norman foundation based on the Benedictine Order of Cluny in France. Dedicated to St Pancras, it occupied the site of a Saxon church (see www.lewespriory.org.uk for more information).

Norman Conquest spread the faith further, with multiple foundations of parish churches, monasteries, friaries and priories, many endowed with considerable estates. These are scattered throughout the Park and include such sites as the priories at Southwick, Boxgrove, Lewes and Wilmington (66), and abbeys such as Titchfield. At Steyning the Normans respected its earlier Christian associations, building their church

67. The now isolated church of Upwaltham in West Sussex. It is early Norman in construction with some Gothic alterations of the 13th to 15th centuries. It must have served a small community – either a village, now vanished, or a scatter of dispersed farmsteads.

probably close to the shrine of St Cuthman, which had become a site of pilgrimage in the 10th century (see image 99).

The legacy of the Church of Rome in and around the new South Downs National Park is an evocative one. Walking around the ruins of once grand priories like that at Boxgrove, or visiting quiet parish churches, such as Upwaltham (67) north of Chichester, or Clayton, shaded below the chalk escarpment south of Hassocks, it requires an effort to imagine just how central such establishments were to daily lives. Monasteries were some of the wealthiest institutions in medieval society. Peasants were sometimes required to work on ecclesiastical land for no payment, and had to give a percentage of their agricultural produce (a tithe) to the Church. In return, the Church provided the only guaranteed way of entering heaven and avoiding purgatory or hell. The rich elite of society also were in thrall to the attractions of the afterlife, but frequently avoided having to suffer any personal deprivation to get there. Instead they occasionally provided chantries in churches and paid monks to pray for their souls after death.

The break with Roman Catholicism during the English Reformation led to the break-up of the large ecclesiastical estates and the establishment of the Church of England. Parish churches throughout the area of the Park were gradually refurbished in a new protestant ascetic, one that eschewed the ornate flamboyance of colourful Catholic statuary and wall paintings and replaced it with more austere fixtures and fittings. The religious persuasion of most people worshipping within our area was Anglican, and in some cases fiercely anti-Catholic, as is remembered in the annual Lewes

68. Lewes on November 5th is a rowdy place, full of torch-lit processions, and is the time to air present grievances, remember past protests, or commemorate those who have fallen in defending their country. The townsfolk form bonfire societies, this flaming brand being that of the Commercial Square Bonfire Society.

69. Jireh Chapel in Lewes is more than 200 years old and originally housed an independent Calvinistic congregation. Now it is home to the Lewes Free Presbyterian Church, one of seven Free Presbyterian Church of Ulster places of worship in England.

Bonfire Celebrations which commemorate, amongst other things, the burning of the Protestant Martyrs (68). Alternative forms of Christian worship, such as those practised by Methodists, Quakers or Baptists, gradually provided some variety in the 18th and 19th centuries, even more so in Hampshire. The Sussex Methodist churches of Ashington (closed 2010), Steyning and Storrington form a downland trio, while those in Winchester and Fareham are examples of the Baptist movement. The Jireh Chapel in Lewes originally housed a Calvinistic congregation (69). But despite the pervasive influence of various forms of Christianity within the Park, old 'superstitions' still persisted, acted out in tandem with the national religion. The occasional find of a shoe, or other object, concealed in the chimney of a country cottage, or the burial

70. The Long Man of Wilmington is thought by historians and archaeologists to date probably to the 16th or 17th centuries. There are many, however, who believe in a greater antiquity for the figure, and consider it has special powers or qualities. Above the figure are a complex of earthworks that probably include prehistoric long and round barrows.

of a witch-bottle, like that from Michelham Priory, is testimony to the enduring fear of the evil eye, and the co-existence of official religion and personal belief.

The modern period, with its rationalism, two world wars, increased social mobility, and its emphasis on commercial and technological progress have shredded the former sense of parish cohesion that once bound communities together, in the Park and elsewhere. With a dwindling number of parishioners, some churches and chapels have become less place of worship, more picturesque historical monument. To the casual visitor, they seem imbued with the religiosity of former times, rather than being epicentres of contemporary religious fervour. New religious establishments in the South Downs National Park, the mosques of Brighton and Winchester, the Chithurst Buddhist Monastery (Thai Forest Tradition) between Midhurst and Petersfield speak both to the effects of globalisation and to alternatives to predominantly western values. As does the continued spirituality of the Long Man of Wilmington (70). In providing the foci for different beliefs and rituals, they continue a tradition in the Park that began some 6000 years ago.

Beliefs, rituals, superstitions and religions all promise some sort of individual and communal spiritual protection. But human beings often require more materialistic and tangible signs of being able to safeguard themselves and their kin. It is these more obvious monuments of shelter and security that we visit next.

Defensive displays

While the archaeological and historical evidence from the South Downs National Park provides plentiful confirmation of the need of human beings to believe in things beyond mortal understanding, there is also equally abundant testimony to demonstrate that there were frequent episodes of physical aggression and protection. The first millennia of occupation in the Park – that by hunters and gatherers, the first farmers and metalworkers – have left little trace of defended strongholds. However, the lack of such sites should not persuade us that life was always peaceful. From elsewhere in the country, and from studies of surviving hunters and gatherers in other parts of the world, the propensity for domestic and community violence is always present. Those flint-tipped hunting arrows or wooden-handled stone axes can also inflict serious injury and death. Perhaps the bouts of fighting were shorter, less organised and not sustained, but it is likely that they existed.

Just before the onset of the Iron Age, around 800 BCE, there is evidence of climatic deterioration – there was more rainfall – making some lands too wet to cultivate. This may

71. The diagonal line across the main image is the remains of a bank and ditch that encloses a large area around Belle Tout lighthouse and Beachy Head. Although not accurately dated most people assume it dates from the Iron Age. How much of the supposed settlement (inset image) has fallen into the sea is unknown.

have significantly waterlogged soils on the coastal plain and in the Weald. Whether this pressure on resources provided an environmental trigger for defensive displays is problematic. However, it is during this period that the first large-scale apparently defensive structures appear in the Park – the hillforts. There are a number of these sites scattered along the Downs, particularly along the impressive north scarp, overlooking the Weald. They stretch from Old Winchester Hill and St Catherine's Hill in the west, through Harting Beacon, Chanctonbury, Wolstonbury and Ditchling Beacon, to Seaford Head and possibly Belle Tout in the east (71). When you visit them today, you see grass-covered earthen banks, pierced by one or two entrances, encircling

72. The hillfort on Wolstonbury Hill, on the north scarp of the Downs, enjoys dramatic views over the Weald. It is assumed to be an Iron Age hillfort although the surrounding ditch lies inside the bank, which is unusual. The grassed perimeter bank is also peppered by small ant hills (see inset image). The interior surface is pock-marked by more recent flint-digging.

turf-covered interiors of varying extent. Don't be lulled by those gently sloping earthen perimeters. In the Iron Age many would have had vertical faces of timber, turf and stone. The hillforts come in all sizes – large (Cissbury); medium-sized (Hollingbury) and small (Caburn). And all shapes – oval (Wolstonbury) to almost rectangular (Harting Beacon) (72).

Describing hillforts is much easier than explaining what they were for. They do seem to be, in part, related to defence and protection. However, studies have demonstrated that some of the so-called defensive earthworks or 'ramparts' are just too oddly sited to have functioned in that way. The northern perimeter of Devil's Dyke seems too far down a precipitous slope to have worked. Display and defence are frequent bedfellows and in many hillforts an impressive demonstration of power through highly visible barriers may have been more important in making a statement to neighbours, than manning them to repel attackers. Excavations within hillforts have clearly indicated that no two are identical – some have evidence for many round-houses and four-post granaries; others for crafts such as metalworking, while some enclose wide and open spaces – for the protection

73. The verandahed white house at Milland sits atop a Roman enclosure formed by a bank and ditch. The ditch can be seen to the right of the house, as can the corner of the enclosure. Thought to be a *mansio* or posting-station it may once have accommodated, fed and watered travelling officials and horses on the road from Chichester to Silchester.

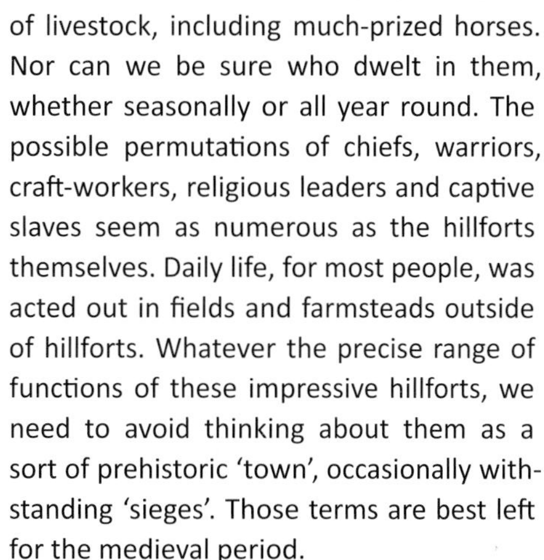

of livestock, including much-prized horses. Nor can we be sure who dwelt in them, whether seasonally or all year round. The possible permutations of chiefs, warriors, craft-workers, religious leaders and captive slaves seem as numerous as the hillforts themselves. Daily life, for most people, was acted out in fields and farmsteads outside of hillforts. Whatever the precise range of functions of these impressive hillforts, we need to avoid thinking about them as a sort of prehistoric 'town', occasionally withstanding 'sieges'. Those terms are best left for the medieval period.

Right at the end of the Iron Age, just before southern Britain became an outlying part of the Roman Empire, large scale earthworks, enclosing vast areas, were constructed north of Chichester (the so-called Chichester Dykes) and in the Winchester area (Oram's Arbour). Again the precise range of activities that took place within these banks is unknown, centres for settlement have not been located. However, it is likely that forms of trade and exchange occurred, probably on a periodic basis. You would think that the advent of Roman legions in 43 CE to southern Britain brought the first proper military camps and forts. It did, but not in the area of the South Downs National Park, apart from later posting stations at Milland (73) (near Midhurst) and Hardham

74. The magnificent remains of Pevensey Castle, just east of the South Downs National Park. The Norman Castle sits within the earlier late Roman walled circuit. Pevensey also saw activity in World War II, housing the Home Guard and American and Canadian troops.

(near Pulborough). The reason for this is quite straightforward. This area of the south coast had long enjoyed productive relationships with northern Gaul and when the Romans arrived there were few pockets of resistance south of the Thames and east of the Solent. The result was that daily life continued much as before, especially in rural areas – the only difference being that previous tributes to a local chief now became taxes to a colonial official. It is true that the Roman administration encouraged town-life, particularly at Winchester and Chichester. How successful these new towns were is debatable. In their first two centuries they did not have masonry town-walls, and were small and under-populated. Although Chichester was surrounded by bastioned walls late in the Roman period, that may have been more do to with perceived threats from sea-borne invaders, rather than a bold statement of urban prosperity (see image 54).

75. Burpham, near Arundel, is one of a series of *burhs* (fortifications) ordered by Alfred the Great or his successor, Edward the Elder in about 800 CE to defend Sussex from the Vikings. This substantial earthen bank defended a large promontory. The Saxon term *burh* is incorporated into the modern placename.

If the area of the South Downs National Park is fortunate, situated in the mildest climatic zone of Britain, covered with thin but fertile soils, and flanked by heavier, but equally fertile terrain – it has one obvious weakness, exploited by aggressors on a number of occasions – proximity to the sea, and to the Continent. The Anglo-Saxon Chronicle records the arrival of Aelle and his sons in 477 CE, and his subsequent attack on *Anderitum* (Pevensey) in 491 CE (74). Waves of Saxon settlers followed, either living in separate settlements amongst the surviving Romano-British population, or occasionally occupying areas by force. The south coast was even in reach of the Vikings for a few centuries. It is only with the battle of Ellingsdean (West Dean – north of Chichester) in 1001 CE that the Vikings make their historical entrance into the Park area, but the defensive stronghold at Burpham (75) on the Arun, a Saxon fort or *burh*, and the re-use of Roman fortifications at Chichester by King Alfred and his son Edward the

Elder, demonstrate that the former sons of Saxon raiders eventually became the fathers of downland defenders. Similar defensive *burhs* were constructed at other locations in or around the Park, including Lewes, Chichester and Winchester. But if the Vikings never managed to settle in the South Downs National Park, their successors – the Normans – certainly did.

The Norman Conquest ushered in the great age of castle building in the South Downs National Park. Castles were a completely novel type of fortification, and permission from the King was needed for their construction. They were much smaller than prehistoric hillforts, Roman towns or Saxon *burhs,* indicating clearly that they were not designed to defend most of the population, but only the new, foreign elite and their families and close associates. The earliest castles, post-1066 CE, are known as 'motte and baileys', essentially earthen mounds topped with timber towers protecting lower courtyards defended by earthworks. Later castles were built in stone. Castles were just not defensive structures, and, in fact, few of them suffered regular siege or assault. Rather they were the bases from which offensive actions could be mounted. They also acted as administrative centres for the new Lords, to whom pledges of loyalty could be made and various feudal services performed. Motte and bailey castles once existed throughout the Park, for instance, at Winchester, Rowland's Castle, Chichester, Midhurst, Edburton and Lewes. The organisation of Sussex was unique in the Norman period, as previously noted. The Downs, and some of the Weald, were divided into six military regions called *rapes*, each one controlled by the castle of a Baron. Major masonry castles therefore developed at Arundel, Bramber (76) and Lewes (all in, or close to the Park) with easterly fortifications at Pevensey and Hastings.

Norman power was exercised both through military might and divine authority so it is no surprise that there was significant ecclesiastical ownership of lands throughout the Park. Nor is it at all extraordinary that fortifications were constructed for the Church. Wolvesey Castle at Winchester was built for the Bishop of Winchester, Henry of Blois, between 1130 and 1140. When control of Normandy was lost in 1204, the English monarchy and prominent Lords and ecclesiastics continued to refurbish many castles and religious foundations in stone. At Winchester Henry III added the Great Hall to the earlier Norman fortification

76. The imposing remains of the Gatehouse Tower at Bramber Castle rise monolith-like above the now grassed interior of a powerful Norman Castle. Founded in 1073 it was furnished within a generation with masonry curtain wall and gates. Adjacent Bramber Church (with its weird carvings) is a surviving part of the same building-complex. In the late 19th century the grounds housed a tea room and occasionally a fairground.

between 1222 and 1235 CE (77). (It now houses a museum of the history of the city.) Increasing tension between France and England from the second half of the 13th century onwards saw a wider proliferation of defensive building, including other types of monument. An impressive Barbican Gate was added to Lewes Castle in the 1340s, while grants to construct town walls were given to Chichester (1261), Lewes (1264) and Arundel (1295). The Bishop of Chichester was granted a licence to crenellate a fortified manor house at Amberley, on the Arun, while priories at Michelham and Wilmington were reinforced, the former with an impressive gatehouse and moat. Warblington Manor House, in south-east Hampshire, was also moated and fortified around this time.

77. Henry III added the Great Hall to Winchester Castle in the first half of the 13th century. A Round Table purporting to be King Arthur's dominates one gable wall, but in reality it was made in the 13th century and was repainted during the reign of Henry VIII. A good example of the use of the early medieval past in the later medieval present.

By 1600 CE castles had become obsolete, along with the use of the long-bow and cross-bow. Instead smooth-bore firearms and the use of gunpowder to fire shot were to provide the technological basis for warfare into the 20th century. Threats, both real and perceived, were still from across, or via, the English Channel, with the French, Spanish and assorted pirates and smugglers the principal culprits. Instead of relying on a collection of feudal Lords for defence, the English monarchy, from Henry VIII onwards, began to devise a system of national defence that resulted in a variety of coastal fortifications and gun batteries to repel seaborne attacks. Crucial to the effectiveness of coastal protection was an early warning system and, from the 16th century onwards, a number of fire beacons (78) were set up along the length and breadth of the Park to warn authorities of potential threats. Coastal defensive buildings varied in date and design and included the Redoubt at Eastbourne (1804), the chain of Martello towers (taking their name

78. Mount Harry was the site of the Lewes Beacon from at least the 16th century. It was part of a defence system for the South Coast and was lit to warn the local militia when invasion threatened from the sea.

79. Shoreham Fort was built in 1857 as part of the defences of the South Coast. Luckily the fort never had to fire its guns in anger and was abandoned for military use in the early 20th century. In 1914 it housed the first film company in West Sussex – The Sunny South Film Company.

from a tower at Cap Mortella, Corsica and constructed from Seaford to Aldeburgh in Suffolk) designed to repel a possible invasion by Napoleon, late 18th-century brick batteries including two at Brighton, and the Victorian forts at Newhaven and Shoreham (79). Barracks for troops to defend the coast against the French were built at Exceat (Cuckmere Valley) in 1804 – some of the foundations and a water trough can still be seen. As the 19th century progressed strategic defence emphasised the increasing role and importance of the Royal Navy, based at Portsmouth, in defending southern Britain from the sea. It was from that port in 1805 that Admiral Nelson sailed for the final time to defeat the Franco-Spanish fleets at Trafalgar, a famous triumph for the nation despite the Admiral's tragic death.

The 20th century, with its two world wars and the ensuing Cold War, has left an indelible historical and archaeological legacy within the South Downs National Park. Some of the Great Houses were commandeered as centres of military recruitment, and never quite recovered their elitist positions afterwards. The military camp at Hazeley Down, Owslebury, now marked by a commemorative granite cross, was one of the last memories of Blighty for many, before they were shipped from Southampton to the muddy chaos of the Somme (80, 81). Newhaven was a pivotal port from which stores were shipped to the battlefields of northern France. The twice-weekly arrivals of wounded from the Front at Brighton Station were harrowing spectacles, and the first hospital for shell-shock cases was established in the town. In 1916 Portsmouth experienced its first aerial bombardment from a Zeppelin Airship. World War II was every bit as

80. This isolated building stands on Hazeley Down, near Winchester, and may mask the framework of one of the World War I camp buildings that housed troops in 1916–17 destined for the front.

81. A memorial on Hazeley Down to World War I troops.

82. About 28,000 pillboxes and other hardened field fortifications were constructed in England in 1940 as part of the British anti-invasion preparations of World War II. About 6500 of these structures still survive, including this one in the Cuckmere Valley. Pillboxes derived their name from their similarity to medicinal boxes for pills.

intensive in its effect on the Park. A complex of pill-boxes (82), machine gun-posts and anti-tank obstacles were deployed, particularly in the Cuckmere Haven where intelligence suggested a potential German invasion (83). A rusting Mark II Churchill tank on Kithurst Hill (south of Storrington) left behind by the 14th Canadian Army is as memorable as it is anomalous (84). Large manor houses again became home to military personnel, as at Stanmer, while that at Bignor was a centre for the French Resistance. Decoy airfields, with false runway lights, such as that at Gumber, near Slindon, were laid out to fool German bombers. Despite heavy bombing during the war the docks and beaches of the Solent provided the springboard for the D-Day landings of 1944.

A walker in the South Downs National Park today, admiring the countryside views, or visiting some of the celebrated but much earlier heritage, can easily overlook many indications of more recent, 20th-century military activity. Odd depressions in the turf may mask former slit-trenches or fox-holes to hide a soldier; brickwork hidden by brambles may signify a pill-box; an incongruous line of concrete may suggest a former anti-aircraft battery. Sometimes this hidden heritage is deliberately deceiving. A slightly isolated, but otherwise ordinary looking bungalow on Truleigh Hill, overlooking the Weald, was designed to be just that – isolated and ordinary – for a good reason. It contained a top-secret intelligence installation during the Cold War. And an underground reservoir at Twyford (near Winchester), only completed in 1990, was designed to protect Southern Water staff, tasked with restoring safe water supplies in the event of a nuclear attack. It was an impressive structure, but thankfully never needed.

83. The Cuckmere Valley in the east of the Park contains one of the rivers that divides the chalk downs into discrete blocks. Classic meanders and several oxbow lakes are a characteristic of the area. The Cuckmere Haven was frequently used by smugglers in the pre-modern period.

84. Archaeology on the Downs does not only consist of the ancient and the grassed-over. This tracked vehicle base on Kithurst Hill was once part of a WWII tank belonging to the Canadian Army. The only action it ever saw was for target practice, hence its pock-marked side.

Keeping in touch with the dead

As I write these words I am conscious that today is Halloween, 2011. The dead have always exerted an enduring influence on the living and today is no different. Not just in the tricksy event that Halloween has become, but also through the power of mediums, or people who claim to be able to speak to the dead. Sometime today in Liverpool a show-stopping celebrity psychic will be offered the chance to demonstrate, in a rigorously controlled setting, rather than a theatrical one, that she can really communicate with the dead. A well-known anthropologist also tells a nice story about the ubiquity of ancestors in parts of Africa. He recalls observing a solitary young boy walking along a dirt road, in animated conversation, seemingly with himself. However, the boy claimed he was arguing with some of the ancestors from the village, chastising them for causing an outbreak of illness amongst the living, and urging them to do something about it. The boy was particularly vehement that he had made all the necessary offerings to the ancestors and kept his side of the bargain. (Later, in an admission to the anthropologist, he admits to short-changing the ancestors in some of his offerings.) But the point of this story is that, in many societies, the spirits of the dead are both real and really rather ordinary; they are often comforting, sometimes threatening, but likely to cause mischief if ignored. Where can we find the ancestors in the South Downs National Park? In some obvious places, such as church graveyards and war memorials, but also under hundreds of ancient earthen mounds that lie scattered throughout the Park. It's time to meet a few of them.

85. The living and the dead can be symbolized by natural things – in this case a mature tree and a dead tree trunk above Plumpton on the Downs. Ancestors might have been personified by the branches of the dead tree, wildly reaching out and remonstrating with the living.

The very first ancestors are difficult to find. Those early hunters and gatherers in the Park, from around 6000 BCE, have left no trace of how they cared for their dead. There are no graves or cemeteries, and no locations where human bones or ashes have been discovered. We must assume that they did treat the death of one of their kind as a special event, requiring specific rites and practices. Not all procedures for disposing of the dead would leave permanent marks on the landscape. It is possible that bodies were burnt and ashes scattered on the winds, or that the dead were ceremoniously propped up against a tree, by a departing band of hunters, and left to slowly dissipate through the forces of nature. As the physical body decayed the tree grew. In such circumstances the tree (85) may even have become the ancestor.

But the truth is, for this period, we simply don't know where the ancestors of those early hunters were, and might still be.

With the first farmers in the Park, the ancestors come into sharper focus. We can visit some of their final resting places in a few surviving long and oval earthen mounds. Within the Park they form two small concentrations, one in the east between Brighton and Eastbourne at sites such as Alfriston, Long Burgh and Windover Hill, one in the west between Chichester and towards Winchester (e.g. Bevis's Thumb (86), North Marden). Beyond the Park boundary, close to Andover, lies the excavated site at Nutbane; our most detailed evidence for the ancestors comes from the latter site. The long mound was trapezoidal in shape, wider at the eastern end, and flanked by ditches from which the chalk for the mound had been derived. It is clear that the first structural elements, prior to the mound, were a series of timber mortuary houses, containing three crouched adult bodies and one of a child, laid out at different times. After an interval the timber houses were deliberately set on fire, and the whole buried by the construction of the long mound. Remains of broken pottery and animal bones from the eastern, or 'forecourt' end, suggest that regular feasting probably took place to honour the dead. The oval barrow at Alfriston covered two pits, one of which contained the crouched burial of a young female. The earlier long barrows near Owslebury (87), and the later oval barrow at Alfriston, must have been prominent landmarks – initially mounds of freshly dug greyish and white chalk. Their construction probably involved many members of the community, who subsequently communicated with the dead by periodically sharing a meal with them. These early ancestors may have been the founding pioneers of some of the earliest farming settlements.

86. Bevis's Thumb Long Barrow lies near the village of Compton in West Sussex. These burial mounds are usually over 5000 years old and might have contained the ancestors of the first farmers in the area. Bevis was a local mythical giant – of truly huge proportions if this is only his thumb.

87. One of the long barrows near Owslebury in Hampshire. Mature trees and fallen leaves now mask this long mound, making it difficult to spot. But 5500 years ago the mound probably stood free of trees, and comprised a long whitish chalk embankment, perhaps with ditches on each long side.

88. In many areas of the South Downs National Park the most numerous archaeological monument are the round barrows, or burial mounds, of the second millennium BCE. This one (near Edburton), immediately beyond the small fence, is typical – in that its central depression shows that it was 'excavated' by antiquarians, probably in the 19th century. The inset image shows a barrow from the group at Petersfield.

89. Round barrows were often thrown up over the ashes from cremated individuals, and the ashes were occasionally contained in large ceramic pots, sometimes buried upside down underneath the mounds. This is one such urn, from a burial at Itford, outside Lewes.

During the millennium of 2500 BCE to 1500 BCE the ancestors multiply considerably in number and their resting places can be identified in the Park by mostly smallish turf-covered round mounds. There must have been thousands of these mounds at one time (88), hundreds scattered along the north escarpment of the Downs, with fine views over the Weald, certainly indicating that the dead were meant to enjoy the scenery as much as the living. They also acted, of course, as very obvious territorial markers. The mounds cover a variety of burial forms, including single inhumations and cremations (with the ashes in large ceramic urns (89)), and several separate cremations. Mounds can be stand-alone or grouped into cemeteries of 'barrows'. Some of the burials beneath the mounds were spectacular. In 1850s an inhumation in a timber coffin at Hove was accompanied in death by an amber cup, a Scandinavian stone battle axe, a whetstone pendant and a bronze dagger – ably demonstrating that connections by sea always linked the Downs to the Continent. A similar tree-trunk coffin was found in the Great Barrow at Bishop's Waltham. There is a concentration of very large mounds in the Chichester region (e.g. the Devil's Humps at Bow Hill) and along the Rother valley, on the greensand, towards Heyshott Down and Petersfield. At some of these sites (e.g. the Devil's Jumps near Treyford (90)) there are barrow cemeteries whose long axes point towards the north-west, probably aligned on the midsummer solstice. This suggests that the ancestors lived in ritual landscapes in the Park area, which were more extensive than their individual barrow locations.

If we use our imaginations we can visualize this ancestral landscape of the Park. Over the 1000 years of round-barrow burial let's assume that some 4000 barrows were thrown up. That equates to about four barrows a year. We do not know where these people were living, and it is quite likely that the majority of mourners lived in settlements outside the Park. Nor do we know where the cremation pyres were sited, or

90. This reconstruction drawing shows the six round barrows that comprise the group known as the Devil's Jumps, near Treyford. The ditches surrounding each barrow can be clearly seen. The mounds appear to be in a line trending south-east to north-west and aligned on the sunset on midsummer's day.

even that the majority of the dead received barrow burial. But by, say, 1500 BCE some of the Park must have been so populated by the dead that it resembled one vast cemetery-landscape, full of older turf-covered barrows, new whitish chalk barrows, funeral pyres, and processions of wailing mourners. All engaged in the very necessary task of keeping in touch with their loved ones. Their ancestors, in return, must have watched over the fields and animals of the living.

In the subsequent Iron Age, from 700 BCE, the ancestors, by and large, disappear. There are one or two isolated burials, such as the crouched inhumation from the Goodwood Estate, near Chichester, but their rarity suggests there is something abnormal about these. People who die 'bad' deaths, such as those who have died from an accident, or as a result of being a witch during life, are often treated as outcasts in death. But what became of most of the dead? One theory is that, as many elaborate weapons of this period are found in rivers, the water-courses and streams of the Park must have swallowed up mortal remains. Some have even suggested that the taboo on fish-eating that seems to have been practised by the living was caused by this method of disposal.

91. The Romans liked to ensure their dead were content – otherwise they would come back to haunt them. These pots are from a cremation burial at St Pancras, Chichester. The hands hold the vessel that contained the ashes, while the other pots are for food and drink to nourish the departed.

There are a few exceptions. A flat cremation cemetery at Westhampnett, just east of Chichester, dating from 100 BCE, contained the remains of 161 individuals. The pottery accompanying them, however, suggests that they were recent immigrants from the Continent. At Owslebury, in Hampshire, a man was buried with a shield, sword and spear – a so-called 'warrior burial'; he may have been the much revered founder of the settlement.

The Romans wanted to control the dead as much as the living. They both respected and feared the ancestors. Near the Park area one of the largest Roman cemeteries is that at St Pancras outside the east gate of Chichester. The estimated surface area of the cemetery in antiquity was some two hectares, and up to 10,000 people could have been buried there between 70–250 CE. On average one person a week, after the cremation rites, would have been interred – a very frequent occurrence which no doubt was noted ominously by most of the inhabitants of the town. Some of the dead, most of them locally born, were accompanied by a variety of jugs and plates from which to eat in the afterlife (91). There were clearly status distinctions to maintain among the dead.

Another early cremation cemetery existed at Alton, while a later urban cemetery of inhumations was excavated at Lankhills, Winchester. Cremation persisted into the early Anglo-Saxon pagan period, and there are a number of early cemeteries between the rivers Ouse and Cuckmere in the east of the Park. At Alfriston the ashes of two of the dead of a small community were placed in distinctive pedestalled pots with bosses on them; however, most were inhumed, males accompanied by a sword, shield or axe, women by elaborate brooches (92). A potential link with the earlier Romano-British population is also evident at the cemetery at Itchen Abbas, near Winchester, which spans the late Roman – early Anglo-Saxon periods.

92. The Anglo-Saxons wanted their dead to look their best. This is a spectacular decorated pennanular brooch from Alfriston dating to the 6th century CE. Mainly worn by women, brooches used in pairs fastened dresses, while single brooches fastened cloaks.

With the arrival of Christianity that long age of ancestral veneration was seemingly coming to an end, to be replaced by a much more organised and controlled worship of a supreme God, and a tradition of east–west orientated inhumation burials. On a small hill at Apple Down, north-west of Chichester, the excavation of two cemeteries demonstrated this transition. The first cemetery, in use until *c.* 700 CE, contained a mix of cremation and inhumation burials, associated with small timber structures covering cremations that may have been 'houses for the dead', or family shrines, visited for generations. The second cemetery, located right on top of the hill, was slightly later and contained nine east-facing inhumations of people who may well have been baptised Christians. Not that all the dead were God-fearing. As a national government emerged and began to tighten its grip on local communities, execution and associated burial sites, like the one on Stockbridge Down, in the Test valley, became more common. Here was the grave of someone who had managed to hide a small stash of pennies from his executioners in around 1065. Another had been put in the grave without his head, as had a dog. Polite 1930s interpretation saw this as man and hound punished for illicit hunting; the more explicit 1990s saw it as punishment for bestiality.

Yet the ancestors haven't simply disappeared. Throughout the South Downs National Park one of the most evocative places to feel the presence of the dead is in the graveyards of its hundreds of parish churches, as well as the associations of the dead with religious institutions such as monasteries, priories, friaries, hospitals and, after the Reformation, chapels. There is nothing quite so emotive as wandering among overgrown graves and discoloured headstones in some country graveyard, trying to decipher their symbolism, names, dates and family relationships, and to

93. The parish church beneath the Downs at Clayton is famous for its medieval wall paintings. These probably date from around 1100 CE and depict the Last Judgement, angels and apostles.

reflect on the sorrows of widows, sons and daughters. There is a different sense of time in these places, an ancestral atmosphere that threatens to become more tangible the longer you linger. You often you exit gratefully through an old lych gate to breathe more easily in the land of the living (93).

Sometimes, when former religious establishments have disappeared, your imagination has to work harder. Under arable fields outside Winchester lies the hospital of St Mary Magdalen, where apparently the leprous dead were laid to rest before the Norman Conquest. Over 100 medieval burials were located at the Hospital of St Nicholas in Lewes (Western Road), long since buried itself by urban buildings. Excavations of part of the cemetery revealed bodies buried in shrouds and coffins. Some were more prosperous, and may have been buried in drier chalk graves, some unfortunate, buried with manacled legs (94), or arms tied behind their backs, suggestive of execution. Life expectancy was short in the medieval period and cemeteries often filled up quickly. Hence the occurrence of charnel pits – where the rested dead were exhumed and re-buried *en masse*. The Hospital of St James and

94. One of the dead from the cemetery of the medieval Hospital of St Nicholas in Lewes. This particular deceased was interred with an iron manacle around his leg. This may be evidence for punishment meted out to him, or his insanity.

95. Many towns and villages throughout the Park have monuments that commemorate the dead of the two world wars. This one at Lewes is topped by a winged female figure carrying a wreathed globe. It was dedicated to the fallen of World War I in September 1922.

St Mary Magdalene, just outside Chichester, was founded as a leper hospital for men in the 12th century, surviving the Reformation by becoming an almshouse for the sick poor. Nearly 400 graves were excavated prior to new building on the site. It was a doomed life, however, as a leper. There was no cure, and indeed if you attempted one you would be thwarting divine will. The benefits came to the carers. If you founded a leper hospital and the inmates prayed for you, your time in purgatory would be lessened.

The 20th century has also left its reminders of the departed throughout the Park. The innumerable war memorials (95) remembering the dead of the two world wars at places big and small, such as Winchester, Hinton Ampner, Rowland's Castle, Chichester, Lewes and Jevington, silently record the suffering of some for the survival of others. During the First World War over 800,000 Indian troops fought for the Allied Powers. King George V wanted some of the wounded Indians to be cared for at Brighton Pavilion, where he hoped the flamboyant Indo-Saracenic architecture would provide appropriate quarters. The bodies of 53 Hindus and Sikhs were taken thence to a location high on the South Downs above Brighton, where a *ghat* (funeral pyre) was built so they could be cremated and their ashes scattered in the English Channel. A small, isolated, tower-like structure, a Chattri – gleaming white Sicilian marble viewed against the brilliant greens and blues of a summer downland morning- now marks the spot where cremation pyres once burned (see image 6). In even more recent times, the dead within the South Downs National Park, like the dead of those very first hunters, are there but unseen. The practice of scattering human ashes is quietly undertaken by mourners. On bright sunlit days or brooding cloud covered ones, in places with views that stretch the eye, or quietly secret spots, ashes are sprinkled and blown like seed. They are special places for those who want to keep in touch with the ones they loved. They make them live in the present. And that is where they join us in our final story.

96. If the South Downs National Park contains England's 'chalk desert in the sky', then the dew-ponds are quite clearly the oases. The need for water made people and animals rub shoulders together, in the present and in the past.

The past in the present

When you go for a ride or walk or run in the South Downs National Park you travel from one place to another – you walk up a hill or down a High Street; you amble along the bottom of a dry valley, or along the top of the chalk escarpment, looking out over the great wooded expanse that is the Weald of England, and occasionally glimpsing a triangle of blue behind you that is the English Channel. Your journey is very much in the present. When you return home you expect things to be pretty much as you left them – and they will be. But the beauty of the South Downs National Park lies in its uncanny ability to make you forget about the everyday that you have momentarily left behind. The here and now becomes blurred by the past and future. Alone, lost in thought, you can easily seek this transcendence and solace in the downland views. Even as a couple, sheltering in a thicket of gorse or hawthorn from a sudden squall of rain, rice-paper close, conversation faltered – that slightly unnerving sense of timelessness steals quietly up on you. In those moments you are at one with the generations past who have lived, worked, worshipped, defended and enjoyed the area we now know as the South Downs National Park.

If you trudge up a deeply-worn track at the edge of the Downs you can pause and imagine the thirsty cowherd driving cattle up to summer pasture, or the impatient shepherd and dog hustling a flock down to the sheep fair. Move aside for the noisy quarry men, sweat-stained and covered in grey chalk dust, loading horse-drawn wagons with blocks of chalk ready for the kilns. At a dew-pond you sense the huddle of animals whose shuffling hoofs have trodden the soil around its perimeter into myriad little water-filled depressions (96). Over your shoulder, in the growing gloom, you think you hear a shepherd, whistling sharply, penning ewes behind hazel hurdles for the night, turning his overnight shelter away from the wind. Just for a second you think you catch the wind-carried laughter of women returning from the fields. There are even echoes of more distant pasts.

Stop and linger by any of the hundreds of round mounds that punctuate the landscape. Like a grammar of past grief they huddle in clusters, or stand isolated as shrub-covered mounds in the middle of ploughed fields. Pause to commiserate with a downcast family burying the ashes of a loved relative in pottery urn. Or idle along the grass-covered banks of an Iron Age hillfort and smell the sweet smoke from a pig-roast and listen to the noisy laughter of the large gathering within. Walk along the now-narrow flinty road known as Stane Street that once connected Chichester to London, occasionally pausing to listen, or move smartly to let a wagon bound for market, laden with sheepskins, pass (97). From the top of a rise marvel at matchstick men on flimsy

97. The Roman road of Stane Street once linked Chichester with London. Now in places it is a mute grass-covered bank. But if you stand still enough for long enough you might just catch the rhythmical beat of Rome's soldiers' feet on its flint and stony surface, steadily louder, ominous and persistent.

98. The Norfolk Arms in Arundel, with its Georgian geometric array of windows and central arch for horse-drawn coaches, must have been a welcome site for weary and thirsty travellers. And for the horses too. Warmth, ale, food, straw and stabling awaited.

wooden scaffolding, hauling blocks of greensand, binding them in to the flinty cobbled corners of a tiny, distant, church.

Do not relinquish your time-travels just because you reach the High Street. Despite the bustle your imagined journey is easier here. You can strip the centuries from the building facades that confront you, like layers of an onion. The elegant Regency or Georgian exteriors (98) are passed by horse-drawn carriages with passengers destined for a night at the local coaching inn. Behind these frontages lie timber-framed medieval town-houses, each room occupied by a different family, some preparing goods for the weekly market. Earlier still are the great castles, priories and friaries, full of people bent on taking your labour in this world ... and saving your soul in the next – your life and afterlife are simply not your own. The few streets are murky thoroughfares – you hang onto your coins in case a cut-purse is about, and hold your nose as a cart full of cess spills and splashes shakily past on its way to the town's ditch.

Just as we can experience the past of the South Downs National Park, so too did other generations who came before us. They each had their own pasts to contend with. Those first farmers who ventured up onto the Downs *c.* 4000 BCE came across deserted woodland clearings, and smouldering camp-hearths of hunters who had seen and heard them coming from afar. Communities burying their dead *c.* 2000 BCE often chose to give them a last resting place under mounds close to the causewayed camps of the earlier farmers, as at Barkhale or Combe Hill, while the builders of Iron Age hillforts, in turn, often enclosed and respected the dead of earlier generations, leaving burial mounds intact within their encircling banks, as at Old Winchester Hill (see image 7). In the Roman period worshippers erected

99. The interior of the church dedicated to St Andrew and St Cuthman at Steyning in West Sussex. The Norman church, which belonged to Fécamp Abbey in Normandy, probably replaced a wooden Saxon church dedicated to St Cuthman. The solid round columns and dog-tooth arcading are characteristic of Norman ecclesiastical architecture.

100. These walls are all that remain today of the magnificent priory of Lewes, nestling beneath the South Downs. At the time of its dissolution under Henry VIII in November 1537 it owned over 20,000 acres of land in Sussex. In 1845 the Brighton–Lewes railway cutting (extreme right edge of image) destroyed most of what survived of the great church, cloister and chapter house.

shrines within old hillforts such as Chanctonbury, while the Saxons often buried their dead in earlier prehistoric barrows. The Normans, brash and organised in life, still ensured that they anchored themselves in local religious traditions, building on the fame of local saints, as at Steyning (99).

The past is, and was, a potent force, to be reckoned and dealt with, often respected, sometimes destroyed, occasionally recreated, but never ignored. Henry VIII knew this well. His agents tore down religious establishments, like Boxgrove, Lewes and Wilmington priories (100), throughout the Park. Whole parish churches were stripped of their rood screens, vestments and relics, and statuary defaced and decapitated, to symbolise the essential purity of the new Church of England. Recalcitrant monks were unceremoniously de-robed. Sometimes a decisive break with the past was required. And sometimes a deliberate link was sought. The parish church at Iping, on the Sussex/Hampshire border, was rebuilt in the 19th century, but purposefully in 13th-century style (101). More idiosyncratically the Gothic and castellated facade of Clayton Tunnel, leading trains under the Downs to Brighton, was finished off with

101. This is the church at Iping, on the Sussex/Hampshire border. Although it looks old, it was actually constructed in 1885 (to replace an earlier church), but was built in the style of the 13th century. The only link with its venerable history is the Norman bell retained in the church tower.

102. Something of the past is remembered by the grand entrance to Clayton Tunnel, which took the railway from Hassocks to Brighton. The entrance was designed by architect David Mocatta and built in 1841. The tunnel keeper's cottage was added around 1850 by an unknown designer. The whole gothic effect draws its inspiration from a much earlier age.

Caen stone, surely a nod to those distant Norman castle-builders (102).

The past is in the present in two other major ways within the South Downs National Park. Most obviously, you can see objects from the past in some of the Park's major museums. Many of these items have been excavated or found by chance in the Park during the last couple of centuries. And many of them are quite extraordinary. Inside Barbican House Museum, next to Lewes Castle, are some of the exquisite brooches and other personal adornments, such as beads, rings and tweezers, found with some of the Anglo-Saxon dead at Alfriston. In Hove Museum you can marvel at the amber cup found in a chiefly burial – made from Baltic amber, and over 3500 years old. The translucent qualities of this exotic object demonstrate that even then the desire for something magical, extravagant and rare was beguiling. At Worthing Museum you can see at first hand some of the products from the earliest flint mines at Cissbury and Harrow Hill, as well as an exceptional 5th-century Egyptian goblet from an Anglo-Saxon cemetery at Highdown. In the museum at Petersfield you can glimpse artefacts from the more recent and local past of the town and surrounding countryside, including the paintings of local town life by artist Flora Twort. In the nearby Rams Walk shopping mall a rather lost shepherd recalls the past importance of sheep to the town (103). Winchester boasts a number of museums: the City Museum concentrates on the Roman and medieval phases of the modern city, while if you fancy yourself in armour, then the Westgate Museum is the place not only to be seen but also feared.

103. This rather forlorn shepherd sits in the middle of a shopping arcade in Petersfield, Hampshire. Mostly ignored by busy shoppers, or climbed upon by children, he is ready to tell you lots of shepherds' tales – if only you have the time to listen.

Museums certainly help to bring some of the *minutiae* of past lives in the Park back to life. Yet their resurrection is never quite complete. The glass cases that enclose most of the objects are an obvious and necessary evil, but they prevent the visitor interacting enquiringly with the displayed items – as in – just how much does that sword weigh? Or what does that collar really feel like? You can only enquire through your eyes, and while they are clearly better than nothing, they can only provide literally and metaphorically one sense of the past. A better appreciation of past lives can sometimes be obtained where museums are constructed around ancient (or replica) buildings – at least you know that the objects in some of the cases have not moved very far from where they were found! Sites such as Butser Ancient Farm (Petersfield) and the Weald and Downland Museum (Singleton) (104) provide imaginative three-dimensional engagements with the past, despite the fact that the buildings are replicas at the former, and have been brought from other locations at the latter. And the brand new museum in Chichester (*Novium*) invites you to feel the heat from a suite of steamy Roman baths.

The final way the past is present in the Park is a little more subtle, but no less real. L. P. Hartley's novel, *The Go-Between* (1953), began with the famous line: 'The past is a foreign country: they do things differently there.' And, of course, in reading this small book, you might well imagine that applies pretty much to past lives in the South Downs National Park. It does, but only to a certain extent. Born in an age where technological changes seem to accelerate year-on-year, and where, in the not-so-distant but seemingly bleaker and alien world of the 1950s, even most of the people looked grey and thinner, it's easy to think of that inevitable march of time as straight, true and utterly transformative. A hurtling rush into the future that leaves the past behind without a backward glance or trace. But the past is always inescapably in the present, as indicated above. And it's also written into our very genes – through repeating cycles of involvement with our environment.

What are those things in the South Downs National Park that repeat, that came, and come, around again? Well, first there were (and are) the seasons of the year – colder in winter, glowing in summer, damper and danker in autumn and invigoratingly fresh in spring. Although moderated by climate change over the millennia, these were much more noticeable to practically every previous generation in the area now designated by the Park. They dictated when animals could be trapped, or crops sown. They governed the movements of herds and flocks on and off the Downs. Most significantly they laid down what you could and could not eat at various times of the year. Hazelnuts, so important a food resource for early hunters and gatherers, were only collected in recent centuries after the feast of St Philbert (August 22nd), hence their colloquial name 'filberts'. Then there were (and are) the cycles of sun and moon vital to all sorts of prehistoric and historic beliefs. In the 14th century the small town physician in Midhurst or Lewes was likely to treat your affliction by first enquiring when your illness took hold, since he needed to work out where the sun and moon were at the time to prepare the appropriate concoction. Then there were weekly cycles – in the medieval period consisting of days to work on the Lord's manor, days to pray, days to trade at market and days to feast or fast. Finally there were (and are) cycles of generations – of births and deaths, marriages and estrangements, foreign journeys and strange smells, home hearths and familiar beds, war and peace.

It is through these differently geared cycles that lives in the past in the South Downs National Park can be understood, certainly different in degree from our own but not in kind. For some 8000 years or so people who dwelt in the Park needed to utilise and manage its resources. They had food to find and farm – hunting, trapping, gathering, planting, harvesting and herding. They needed buildings to live in, and places to congregate, socialize, feast, joke and love. At times they had to defend their livelihoods from threats, both near and far. More often than not they clung to supernatural beliefs which would bring them good fortune or protect them from harm. And, when breath itself had failed, they created monuments for the afterlives for the dead and invented traditions to ease the pain of passing and the grief of those left behind. And we, too, do all these things. Not really so much time's straight arrow then, but time's continuous spiral, shifting in circles but ultimately repetitive – linking the past with the present, and with the future (105). The past might appear superficially to be a distinctive, foreign country, but lived experiences of ordinary lives provide innumerable elements of continuity. The magic of these stories lies in their combination of the foreign and familiar.

104. The market-hall from Titchfield in Hampshire, now reconstructed in the Weald and Downland Museum. Dating from the 17th century it was rescued by the Museum in 1971. Goods were sold beneath the arcade on the ground floor, while the upper floor housed the Town Council Chamber.

105. The past is all around us. Walkers now stride along the earthen bank of the Iron Age hillfort on St Catherine's Hill, above Winchester. Woad-painted warriors on the same spot may once have looked out on cattle grazing in the river valley below. Now it is a grassed way for a pleasant Sunday morning stroll.

How to find out more about the archaeology of the South Downs National Park

It's pretty easy really. Read a few relevant books in your local library, and look at some of the main websites. Often these will have bibliographies and further reading lists so you will be surprised at how quickly you can amass a lengthy list of works you could look at. A few books and websites are listed here to get you started. Then go out into the Park and visit some of the major sites. Don't forget to visit your local museum. You will soon become an expert! And, if you really want to get involved, join one of your local archaeological or historical societies.

Visiting Sites

The South Downs National Park is unusual among National Parks in having a relatively minor percentage of its area in public ownership. However, there are plenty of actual historic and archaeological sites in public or charitable ownership that you can visit, and the whole Park is well served by footpaths and other trails. The locations of some of the major sites are indicated on the large map of the Park in this book. For a few of the principal archaeological or historic attractions, like Bignor Roman Villa, or Petworth House, there is an admission charge to pay. For most, like Old Winchester Hill, Hampshire or Devil's Dyke, near Brighton, access is free. The South Downs Way will also take you close to some of the Park's key monuments.

Remember when you visit the Park do follow the good common sense outlined in The Countryside Code – www.naturalengland.org.uk. Make sure you wear sensible clothing and footwear, and carry gloves and a hat – suffering from wind-chill on the Downs can take the edge off the beauty of the scenery! And always carry a compass, a map (the Ordnance Survey Explorer Range at 1:25,000 is excellent) and a mobile phone. GPS instruments are very useful, especially in conjunction with maps, and also have the advantage of working in areas of the Park where there is no mobile phone signal. If you are going to be out for some time – carry a rucksack with water, sandwiches and a flask of something hot.

Books

The South East to AD 1000 – P Drewett, D Rudling and M Gardiner, 1988

The South East from AD 1000 – P Brandon & B Short, 1990

An Historical Atlas of Sussex – eds K Leslie and B Short, 1999

AD43 – The Roman Invasion of Britain – J Manley, 2002

A Review of Archaeology in Hampshire 1980–2000 – ed N Stoodley, 2002

The Archaeology of Sussex to AD 2000 – ed D Rudling, 2003

The South Downs – P Brandon, 2006

The South-East – B Short, 2006

The Archaeology of Fishbourne and Chichester – ed J Manley, 2008

Note also the 150 or so volumes of the *Sussex Archaeological Collections* published by the Sussex Archaeological Society (Lewes). These books, available in most main libraries or by becoming a member of the Society, contain innumerable articles on archaeological and historical sites and themes within the Sussex part of the area now designated the South Downs National Park.

Websites

www.sussexpast.co.uk – The Sussex Archaeological Society covers the whole of Sussex with walks and talks for members/non members, and hosts events at its properties open to the public, such as Michelham Priory and Fishbourne Roman Palace.

www.english-heritage.org.uk – the national site for England's heritage. Contains a very good section on the archaeology of the South Downs National Park.

www.pastscape.org – website of the National Monuments Record. Provides details of many sites featured in this book.

www.bandhpast.co.uk – history project on the parishes of Barcombe and Hamsey in East Sussex.

www.highweald.org/home/weald-forest-ridge.html – includes material on the history, archaeology and built heritage of the Wealden Forest Ridge. Not in the Park but useful as a contrast and counterpart.

www.southdowns.gov.uk – lots of info on the new South Downs National Park.

www.fieldclub.hants.org.uk – the website of the Hampshire Field Club and Archaeological Society.

www.archaeology.co.uk – the UK's most popular magazine for archaeology.

www.britarch.co.uk – Council for British Archaeology – a magazine, lots of information on local archaeological societies – and plenty more!

www.airscapes.co.uk – more of Russ Oliver's dramatic photographs from the air.

www.phocuspocus.co.uk – more of Simon Goodman's imaginative images, especially of the Lewes area.

www.timetalks.co.uk – contact the author of this book to give a talk, or lead a walk, in the South Downs National Park for your Group or Society.

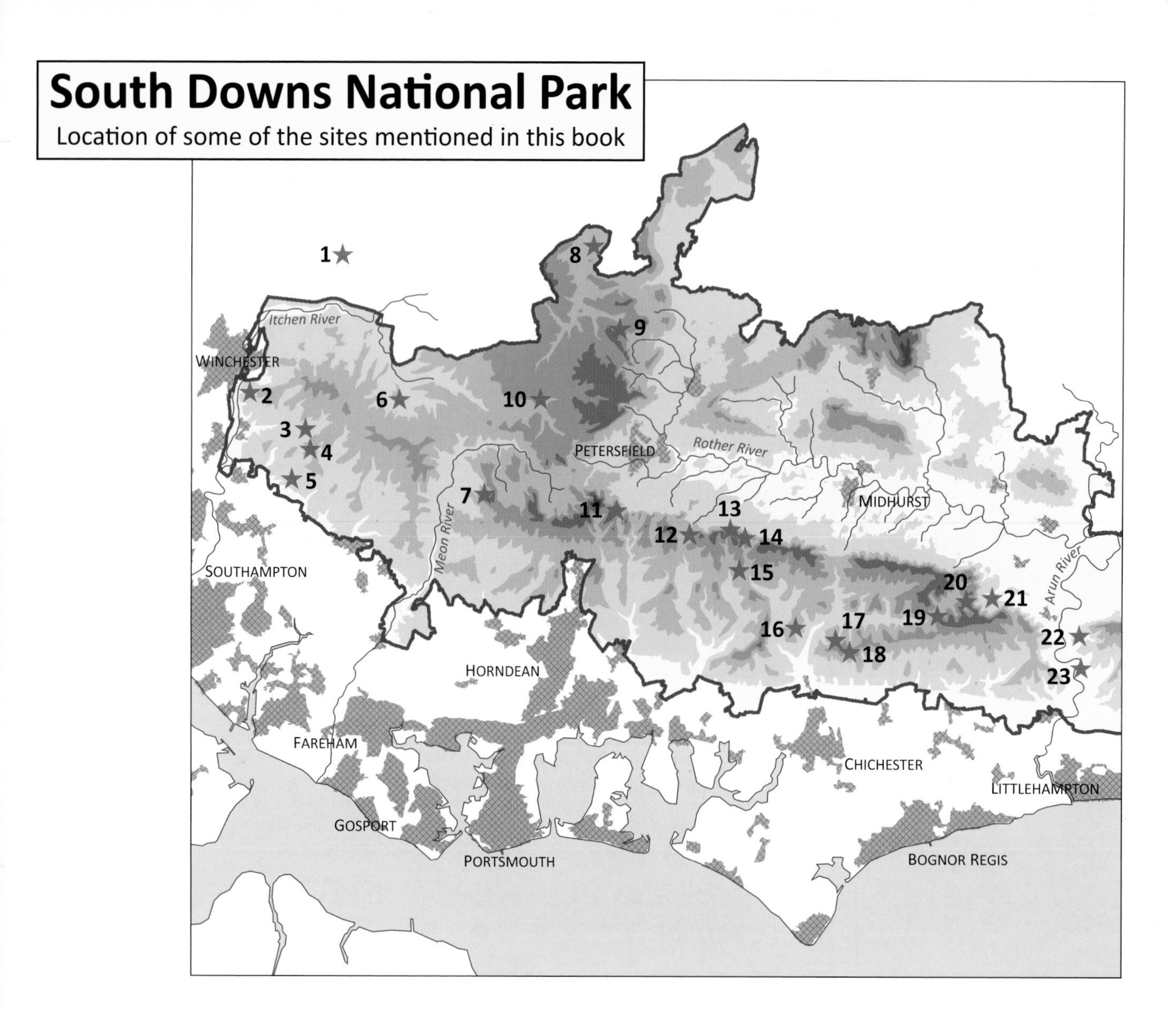
South Downs National Park
Location of some of the sites mentioned in this book
1
2
3
4
5
6
7
8
9
10
11
12
13
14
15
16
17
18
19
20
21
22
23
Itchen River
WINCHESTER
PETERSFIELD
Rother River
MIDHURST
Meon River
Arun River
SOUTHAMPTON
HORNDEAN
FAREHAM
CHICHESTER
LITTLEHAMPTON
GOSPORT
PORTSMOUTH
BOGNOR REGIS

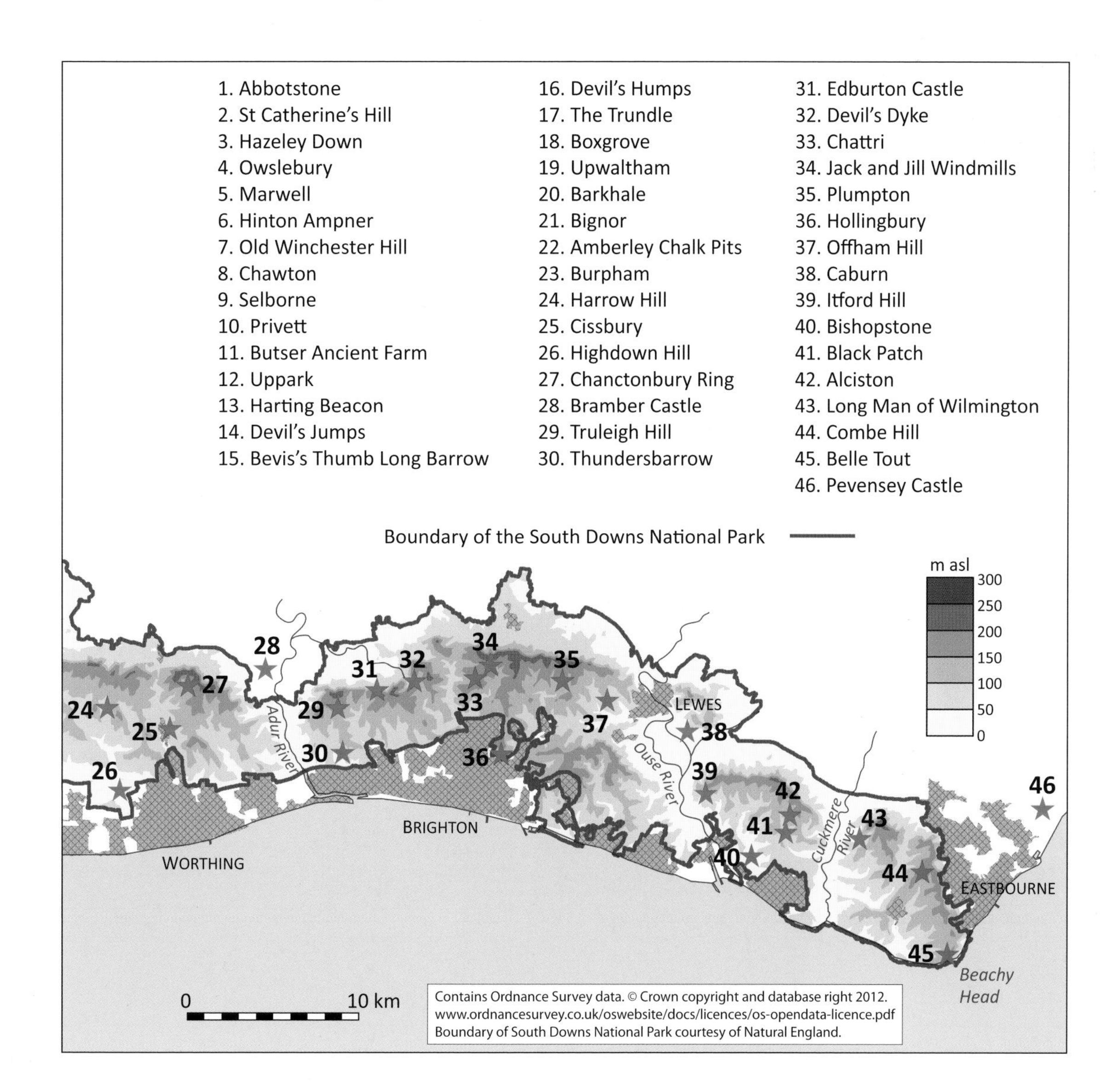
1. Abbotstone
2. St Catherine's Hill
3. Hazeley Down
4. Owslebury
5. Marwell
6. Hinton Ampner
7. Old Winchester Hill
8. Chawton
9. Selborne
10. Privett
11. Butser Ancient Farm
12. Uppark
13. Harting Beacon
14. Devil's Jumps
15. Bevis's Thumb Long Barrow
16. Devil's Humps
17. The Trundle
18. Boxgrove
19. Upwaltham
20. Barkhale
21. Bignor
22. Amberley Chalk Pits
23. Burpham
24. Harrow Hill
25. Cissbury
26. Highdown Hill
27. Chanctonbury Ring
28. Bramber Castle
29. Truleigh Hill
30. Thundersbarrow
31. Edburton Castle
32. Devil's Dyke
33. Chattri
34. Jack and Jill Windmills
35. Plumpton
36. Hollingbury
37. Offham Hill
38. Caburn
39. Itford Hill
40. Bishopstone
41. Black Patch
42. Alciston
43. Long Man of Wilmington
44. Combe Hill
45. Belle Tout
46. Pevensey Castle
Boundary of the South Downs National Park
m asl
300
250
200
150
100
50
0
LEWES
WORTHING
BRIGHTON
EASTBOURNE
Beachy Head
Adur River
Ouse River
Cuckmere River
0
10 km
Contains Ordnance Survey data. © Crown copyright and database right 2012.
www.ordnancesurvey.co.uk/oswebsite/docs/licences/os-opendata-licence.pdf
Boundary of South Downs National Park courtesy of Natural England.

Simplified geology of the South Downs National Park

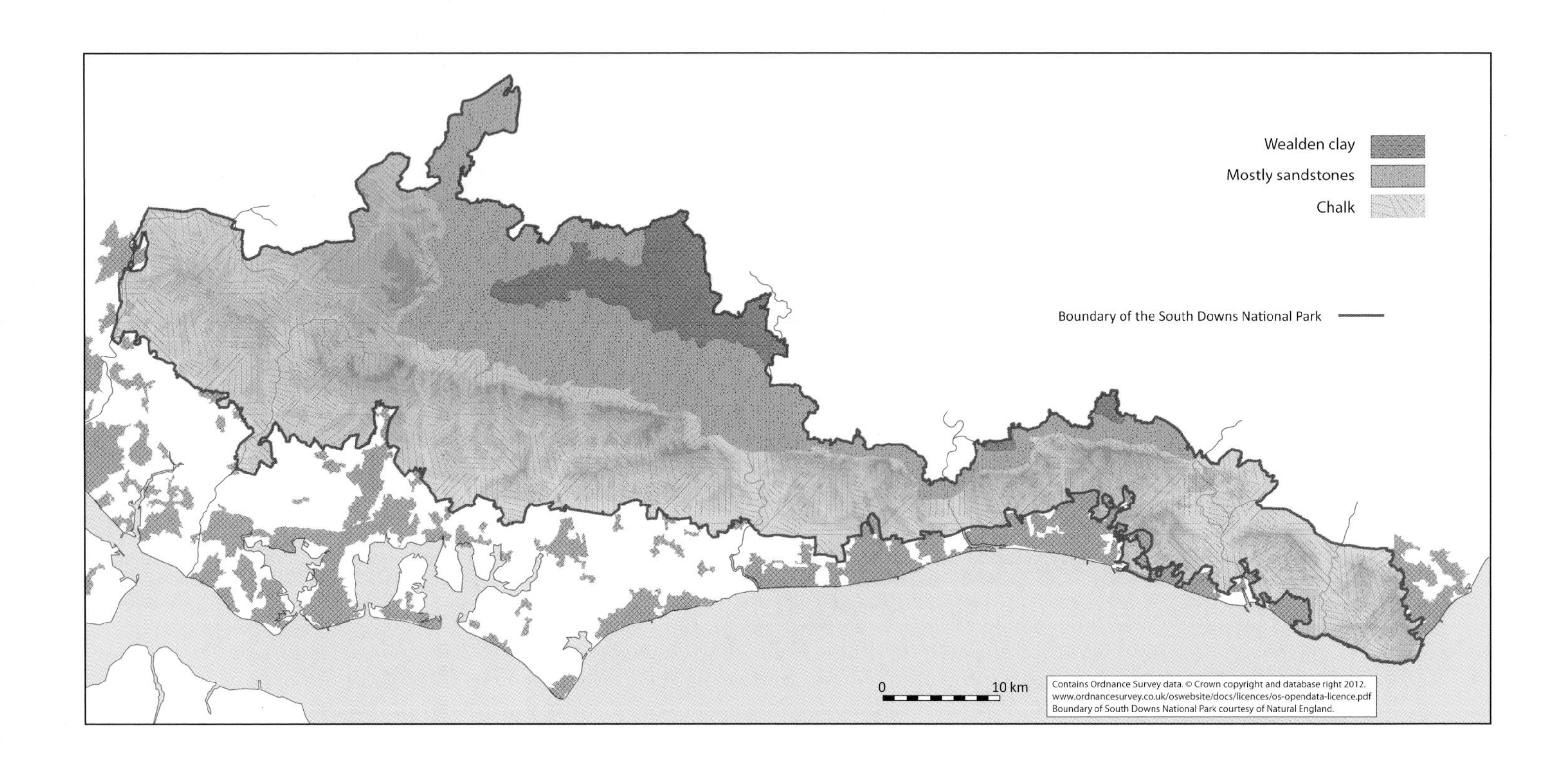

Index of locations and sites